To Deirdre,
All the best!
[illegible]

To Deirdre
Magically
[illegible] '04

Best Wishes
[illegible]

To Deirdre–
Believe in Magic!
[illegible]

Deirdre,
Love,
[illegible]

Other Brookledge Books

Milt Larsen's Magical Mystery Tour of Hollywood's Most Amazing Landmark:
The Magic Castle®
Written, Photographed by Carol Marie

Hockmann, the Great Exposes Himself!
And Other Phony Magicians and Vaudevillians
Written by Milt Larsen, Illustrated by Paul Butler

Hollywood Illusion: Magic Castle®

By

Milt Larsen

First Printing, ©2000
Printed in Canada by
Hignell Book Printing
488 Burnell, MB, Canada
1-800-304-5553

Library of Congress catalogue card number: 00—091917

Front Cover: A James Gallivan graphic photo in a 1924 gold Tiffany desk pad frame from Milt Larsen's desk set.
Back cover: A Clark James graphic photo of the William Larsen, Jr. Memorial Rose Garden.

Cover design by Joe Hoffman

Brookledge Corporation
7001 Franklin Avenue
Hollywood, CA 90028
323-851-3443

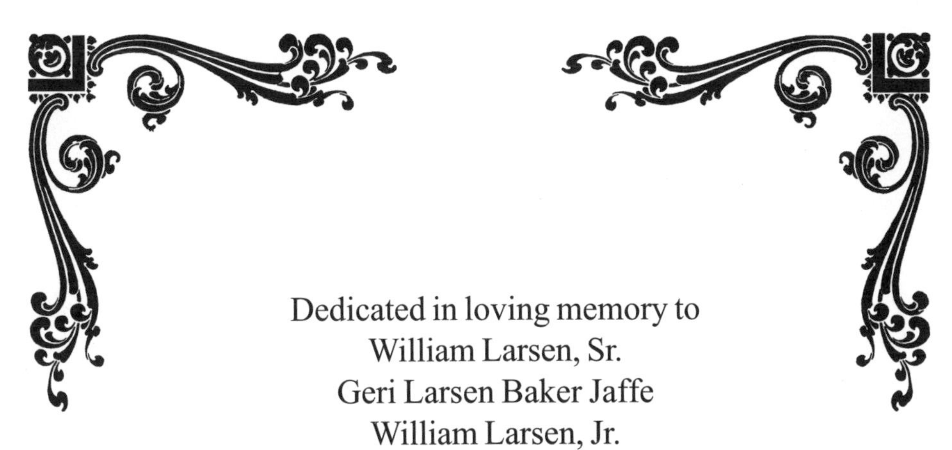

Dedicated in loving memory to
William Larsen, Sr.
Geri Larsen Baker Jaffe
William Larsen, Jr.
and to the members who helped make the dream of a private magic club become a reality.

Acknowledgements: many, many thanks to Bob Busch and Scott Berry, Issa Afram, Victoria Devitt, James Gallivan, Allan Hayden, Joe Hoffman, Clark James, Woody and Tina Kane, Chris Zamiara, Ron Stark & Mary Ann Carey who doctored our vintage photographs at S/R Laboratories in Westlake Village, Marc Wanamaker and Bison Archives for vintage photographs of the Castle and Capitol Records for their permission to use the Witchcraft Magic LP.

Editor's Note

I was fortunate to meet the Larsen family early into my membership at the Magic Castle®. In an effort to learn and understand where and what everything was in the Castle, I took numerous tours with Milt. I, on my own, began taking notes and translating Milt's taped explanation of all the wondrous décor for my own use. One evening, after one such tour, Milt and I ended up sitting together at the Grand Salon bar. He was intrigued at the number of times I had taken the tour and was curious. I replied that I was fascinated with the history and the origins of the original structure and what the Magic Castle® had grown into. I spent hours listening to Milt and his many stories and anecdotes about the evolution of the Castle, the people who helped along the way, incidentally or purposefully.

It was from there our relationship grew. I felt comfortable and protected in what I call my second home. I liked the ambiance, I liked the people I met there, and I enjoyed the wonder of the magic, I enjoyed the company of Milt, The Redeemer. That night, Milt opened a door for me–asking me to write the tour book for everyone. "Just like that?!" He replied, "Just like that!" That *Open Sesame* door mysteriously opened to reveal an even more wonderful world of the Larsens.

A wonderful, albeit strange, relationship with one of the founders of the Magic Castle® had unfolded. I regret that I, unfortunately, never got to know Bill. I was blessed to meet Geri one day in Santa Barbara and found her, at the age of 91, remarkably alert, excited to have a guest, and only hampered by her failing body. She graciously signed my numbered copy of the Tour Book and talked about her love of magic and the Castle.

The Magic Castle® is a special place for me. I have since spoken to many people at the Magic Castle® that feel, as I, that this wondrous magical mansion is their second home as well! Members have told me how having the Castle in their lives has saved them … literally. The Club has aided many people through troublesome times. My experiences with the members of the Castle and the Larsens have been rich. The friends I have made and the times shared are truly memorable. And I can only hope that we will have many more magical times in the future!

Carol Marie

Forward

The interesting thing about a book's Forward is that it is usually the last thing a writer writes before a book goes to press. I fondly call Carol Marie "The Barracuda" because, once she gets her teeth into a project, she will never let go. Like many writers, I am a procrastinator. If there is a deadline for a script or a column I'll make it ... no deadline, I'll put it off forever. Carol Marie set the deadlines and because of her you now have a book in your hand.

I was only thirty years old when I met Tom Glover and conceived the Magic Castle®. I will be seventy years old in the year 2001. I still feel like that same kid (give or take a wince or two caused by falling off ladders along the way.) The Castle still gives me the thrill of a brand new challenge each and every day. It's my fun little tree house where the party has been going on, non-stop, for four decades!

This book is a collection of stores written over the years as part of our Friday Lunch Menu. Every member of the club could write a book about their own anecdotes and remembrances about the Castle, wonderful stories about the Castle and its members could fill the pages of hundreds of books. Within these pages you will simply find some stories that I have enjoyed telling. There is no end to the Magic Castle® story because, as we enter the new millennium, the club is just beginning. The club can never grow old because the entire world of magic is based on new ideas and new concepts. As we go through life in magic the kids become the teachers who will teach new kids so they, in turn, can go on to teach other generations.

My thanks to all the members who have supported my dreams over the years—it has been a great ride.

Milt Larsen

Table of Contents

Pre-opening
A Voyage Without a Map

It all started as a showboat

Many people have no idea that the Magic Castle® started as a *showboat*. The year was 1960. I was writing gags for Ralph Edward's *Truth or Consequences* on NBC-TV. Brother Bill was an Associate Producer at CBS-TV with Don Gotschall. Don got wind of a San Francisco/Oakland ferryboat that was for sale. The price was really cheap. We both thought it would be a great idea to buy the steamer ferryboat and turn it into an old-time showboat. I had already had some success with producing *It's Magic!* at the Wilshire Ebell Theatre in Los Angeles. I loved old-time variety and I could visualize the good ol' Cotton Blossom with a calliope on the upper deck, beckoning people to the theatre for an evening of magic and vaudeville. It's still not a bad idea.

We found a perfect location at a brand new development called Marina del Rey. The Marina had its own share of start-up problems ... something about tides and swamps! Obviously, the Marina would *never* make it! Remember this was 1960. And now, of course, the Marina is some of the most expensive real estate in Southern California.

Even in the early 60's, it wasn't easy to tow a bay-area ferryboat to Los Angeles. And suddenly, the cost suddenly wasn't *that* cheap. Don and I started talking to some developers at Newport/Balboa Bay. They offered us a great location but the logistics of relocating the showboat were staggering … insurance, sewers, permits, harbor environmentalists, and on, and on. Obviously we had a great idea in dreamland but the costs were not realistic. Our dream to become theatrical/restaurant entrepreneurs was simply not getting anywhere.

Don continued to pursue the idea, but I was getting antsy. After all, I was almost thirty years old! Life was passing me by! Maybe we should look for something else. My thoughts always turned to magic. I was the youngest member of the Larsen Family of Magicians. I was the cute, little kid that upstaged my father, William W. Larsen, Sr., on every show (under his expert direction, I might add.)

In 1955 just before Dad passed away at the age of forty-eight, he drove me to the nightclub, Club Crescendo, on Hollywood's famous Sunset Strip. He was doing some legal work for the owners and suggested they turn a back room into a venue for magicians. He might even tie it into the Academy of Magical Arts and Sciences, which he had formed as a *Genii* Magazine promotion in 1951. Dad died before any plans could be put into effect. Somehow, almost ten years later, I seemed to be thinking the same thoughts.

As a writer on *Truth or Consequences*, my office at Ralph Edwards Productions was on the 9th floor of a building at Highland and Hollywood Boulevards. It overlooked a vista of the Hollywood Hills. There was the Yamashiro Restaurant at the top of the hill and directly below was an old hillside mansion. It was very much like those wonderful houses Charles Addams liked to picture in his cartoons, surrounded by weeded grounds.

I used to daydream that a place like that old house would make a perfect magic restaurant. I had asked people about the property and the answers had always been the same: "It's part of a big estate. A developer has bought it and it's going to be torn down." "The city has condemned it. Don't bother." ... "It's not for sale ... Go away, kid, go away!" Ironically, it was the twelve-story building that housed my 9th floor office that was torn down in 1999. (In the year 2002, it will be the exciting new home for the Academy Awards© of the Highland/Hollywood entertainment project.)

One day I was talking to a real estate broker about an old mansion near the Wilshire Ebell Theatre. The mansion was in an R-1 residential zone. It was a great house but the wrong zoning. The conversation led to what kind of a place I was seeking. I said, "There's this great old Gothic Castle on Franklin Avenue in Hollywood." The broker asked, "What's wrong with that one?" I said, "It belongs to a maniac developer who's going to tear it down. It isn't available." The broker countered, "I know the owner. He's not a maniac but I don't think he knows what he wants to do with the house. Why don't you meet him and tell him what you have in mind?" He set up a meeting.

The day I met Tom Glover I was twenty-nine years old. I was a TV game show writer born in Pasadena, California. Tom was in his early fifties. He was a self-made, very successful businessman. Tom was a Texan who wore a Stetson hat and cowboy boots. He had been a football player at Stanford. I told him about all the important people I knew and this idea about a club for magicians. Tom said he hated Hollywood phonies. I replied, "In that case, Mr. Glover, all I have to offer is an idea and a lot of imagination. If nothing else, I'll fix up your building for you." He still wasn't exactly buying it.

At the time, Tom was trying to make large plate glass windows rise and lower mechanically at his Yamashiro Restaurant that he owned. The Yamashiro is the fabulous old mansion at the top of the hill overlooking Hollywood. He had spent a lot of money but the windows still wouldn't open. I invited him to *Brookledge*, our family home where my Brother Bill and later, his wife Irene, resided. I had my theatre/townhouse apartment behind the main house at Brookledge where I showed Tom my homemade Cinemascope screen that rose out of the stage floor at the push of a button. It worked on two surplus bomb hoists and a Sears Roebuck motor. The total cost? It was under a hundred dollars. Now Tom was impressed.

Tom Glover and I shook hands in a Texas-style agreement in September of 1961. With that handshake we entered into a strange and wonderful partnership. Tom entrusted the house to me rent-free and gave me the right to saw, hammer and paint to my heart's content for a year. He would take a percentage of the gross income of the food and bar sales if the place should ever open. The Magic Castle® was a dream on its way to becoming a reality.

That day I called Don and asked him to meet me at Nickodell's Restaurant, the popular radio/TV hangout behind the NBC and CBS Studios at Sunset Boulevard and Vine Street. I told him about my meeting with Tom Glover and suggested that restoring an old mansion in Hollywood was easier than restoring a San Francisco ferryboat. Among other things, the sewage would always flow downhill! (That was a statement that haunted me in later years. Sewage flows anywhere it wants to flow!) Don agreed and we decided to scuttle the showboat.

Haunted House Bar & Grill

Initially, Don and I envisioned a magical haunted house theme bar and restaurant. We quickly learned that the property was in an R-5 residential zone. This meant it could only be a hotel with a dining room and bar or a private club. Suddenly the idea of resurrecting our Dad's dream for a club devoted to the art of magic seemed like a natural way to go. I discussed the plan with my Brother Bill. He loved the idea and agreed to take on the enormous task of creating and organizing the Academy of Magical Arts.

To paraphrase those old Mickey Rooney—Andy Hardy epics: "Gee, Bill. I've found this great old house and we know all these magicians– and our friends at NBC and CBS love bars! Let's put on a show!" Bill and I figured, with any luck, some day we might be able to attract as many as four or five hundred members.

Don and I formed a partnership, Golar Enterprises. Don was able to put up the money that would be needed to get a liquor license and I would take on the day-to-day expenses of restoring a mansion. Obviously, we had absolutely no idea of the costs that lurked ahead. We didn't have time to do a feasibility study–we'd just slay the dragons as they came.

Don was making a decent, but not a huge salary at CBS-TV and I was making a modest salary writing for Bob Barker's *Truth or Consequences*. We were not exactly a team of financial giants. On the other hand, we were two young bachelors with some very exciting dreams.

Don had gotten to know a young attorney with the prestigious Los Angeles law firm of Gibson, Dunn and Crutcher. His name was Bob Post and he was technical advisor for *The Verdict is Yours*, a CBS show on which Bill Larsen was Associate Producer. Bob loved the idea of the Magic Castle® and volunteered his legal services in setting up the new Academy of Magical Arts, Inc.

As Bob rose higher and higher in the ranks at Gibson, Dunn and Crutcher, he remained our legal advisor. A dozen years or so later, my old friend and personal attorney, Gerald M. Singer graciously volunteered to take over the Castle's legal affairs but Bob remained a loyal and active member until his untimely passing.

Gags, Magic and Sawdust

The Magic Castle® probably would never have happened if I had been anything other than a television gag writer with a love and understanding of magic. In comedy writing, nothing is too absurd. In magic, *nothing* is impossible. I never gave much thought to the fact that we were facing an enormous and seemingly impossible task. I simply looked at it as a fabulous opportunity to create something magical. I considered the whole idea more of a theatrical scenario than a business venture. Another part of the combination was a fact that I had a great love for woodworking and carpentry.

My grandfather, Samuel A. Conrad, was a cabinetmaker and carpenter. I had learned a great deal simply watching him at work. When I was a kid, I used to watch the legendary Floyd Thayer turn billiard balls on his lathe in his shop at the Thayer Studio of Magic. Mr. Thayer taught me the basics of wood turning. We used to visit the Thayer plant on San Pedro Street and I watched master craftsmen Carl and Emmett Owen at work.

The Thayer Studio became our own home when my Dad bought the Thayer business and we traded houses back in 1942. His shop became my shop and at twelve years of age, I could turn a respectable walnut multiplying-thimble. At the time we started the Castle, I had built a fairly decent cabin on five acres of homestead land out in the boondocks … now dangerously close to Palm Springs. Some people like to relax by playing golf; I relax by building things.

Another factor that led to the formation of the Magic Castle® was the influence my childhood had on me as part of the Larsen Family of Magicians. My Dad, William Larsen, Sr., gave up the successful practice of criminal law in the late thirties to play the finest resort hotels and clubs with our full evening family show. When I was a little kid at the end of the depression, we lived in Castles. As performers, we lived like royalty in places like the Casa d'Manana in La Jolla, the Del Coronado in San Diego, and the El Mirador in Palm Springs. I loved the gold-painted ceilings and magnificent chandeliers. I have always said I was born with a silver spoon in my mouth—not our spoon, but a silver spoon.

Then we moved into a wonderful home in the Wilshire district of Los Angeles that was something of a Castle itself. *The Brookledge*, as the estate was called, featured a natural stream that was spanned by a complete working magic theatre. Even before we moved there in 1942, our dad would take us to the Thayer Studio almost every Saturday. Like the Castle today, Thayers was a hangout for magicians visiting Southern California. Thus I grew up in palaces, peopled by some of the most famous magicians of the 30's, 40's, and 50's.

When the business out-grew the studio in the residentially-zoned studio, it moved to stores on La Brea Avenue, but the Brookledge was still the place where magicians met. When the Castle opened in 1963 a joke around town was that the Larsen kids had simply moved their magic parties to a place where they could have a cash register. Bill and I grew up in magic and every step of my life seemed to lead to 7001 Franklin Avenue, Hollywood, California, USA. It had to happen!

September 1961—The Beginning

That legendary Texas handshake deal I made with Thomas O. Glover was in September of 1961. Bob Post went to work on the legal part of putting together the lease/sub-lease deals and forming a new California Corporation, The Academy of Magical Arts, Inc. Bill first announced the Castle in the pages of *Genii* Magazine in April 1962. Bill would resurrect the fraternal organization "dedicated to the advancement of magic without politics." I would create a physical, magical fun house in Tom Glover's old Gothic mansion.

The first members were friends who went along with this slightly crazy scheme. About half our members came from the world of magic, who shelled out thirty-five dollars for a paper card and a promise of a place for magicians to hang out. The rest were Bill's cronies from CBS-TV where Bill was gainfully employed as a production executive, and my friends from NBC-TV and co-workers on *Truth or Consequences* and other Ralph Edwards television shows.

The non-magicians plunked out twenty-five dollars for the initiation fee. No one really thought the Castle would make it, but what the hell, I was thirty years old, had three days off between *Truth or Consequences* TV tapings and needed the exercise. Bill had access to the CBS mimeograph machines and pumped out newsletters. It was a crazy idea ... but it just might work.

It immediately occurred to Bill, Don and myself, while sipping at Kelbo's watering hole across from CBS-TV City, that the very first priority in a club for magicians would be the bar. At the time, the three of us thought ABC was just a TV network we didn't work for. We found out the hard way there was another ABC ... the California Alcoholics Beverage Commission. Having a bar was one thing, having a license was another. It was a complicated and expensive process. At that time, as it is today in California, the best way to get a license was to buy an existing one rather than count on a yearly state drawing. We bought our license from the famous old "House of Murphy" restaurant on La Cienega's restaurant row.

Storm Clouds

We posted the required *Notice of Intention* in the front window and I started building the bar. I figured I had about two months to build the Magic Castle®. The notice had to be posted for forty-five days. It would be issued if there were no objections. A representative from the Alcoholic Beverage Commission came by and said we had to re-post the notice on a sign that could be read from the sidewalk.

The future Magic Castle® was a dilapidated old Charles Addams-ish Gothic Victorian mansion surrounded by waist high weeds where there once was a front lawn and rose garden. Take a look at the early photo and you'll get an idea of what the neighbors saw. You have to remember this was 1962. It was the time for hippies, flower children and coffeehouses. It wasn't exactly re-assuring that the name on the notice was "Academy of Magical Arts, Inc." … probably weird and wacko witches and warlocks. Could this spell delays and troubles for the Magic Castle®? You're damned right it could!

We had talked to the manager and general bouncer at the popular Gay 90's restaurant on La Cienega about being our manager. Irvin "Frosty" Frost was a gregarious Irishman who could make you feel welcome as he was physically throwing you out into the street. Frosty can be seen in action these days at The Palm saloon on Santa Monica Boulevard.

One day Frosty was helping me lift my newly constructed back bar into place. A feisty little man burst through the front doors. He demanded to know what was going on. In a volley of four letter words, he introduced himself as Mr. Lipshultz ... the owner of the Biltmore Apartments down the street on Orange Drive. He sputtered that he would make sure we would never get a liquor license. He didn't exactly say he would keep Franklin Avenue "safe from you and your kind" but you get the drift. He made the mistake of questioning Frosty's masculinity with two words that both started with "F." This aroused Frosty's bouncer instincts and Lipshultz found himself "bounced" all the way from our front door to Franklin Avenue.

Next, we found major community leaders and all the churches were opposing our liquor license application. Because of this, we had to go through a hearing process. Suddenly the word was out. The churches in the immediate area protested the granting of the license. After all, the Magic Castle® could be a weird cult of witches and evildoers selling booze, dope and God-knows-what!!! Mr. Lipshultz had done his job. Even Homer Toberman, whose father Charles Toberman started Hollywood, filed a complaint. Apparently I would have a lot more time to hammer and saw.

By the time our hearing came before the Alcoholic Beverage Commission, we had been able to talk to most of the neighbors. Believe it or not, in those days, we did have integrity. Brother Bill was publishing the family *Genii* Magazine and was a very successful TV executive. I had produced *It's Magic!* stage shows for six years and was writing for one of Hollywood's most prestigious companies, Ralph Edwards Productions. Somehow, our neighbors finally figured out that neither of us fell into the weird or wacko cult class. Our neighbors became our greatest friends.

When Bill and I arrived at the ABC hearing, none of the protesters were there ... except, of course, Mr. Lipshultz. He was cursing obscenities between puffs on a large smelly cigar. The dignified hearing officer politely asked Mr. Lipshitz ... er ... Lipshultz to refrain from swearing and to observe the "No Smoking" sign in the hearing room. We all sat back and watched a man being swallowed into a whirlpool of his own making.

The hearing officer finally asked the sputtering, smoking and swearing Mr. Lipshitz ... er ... Lipshultz to leave the room. Our license was approved. We owe a lot to Mr. Lipshultz. His actions delayed the opening of the Castle about one year. It was valuable time we needed and time we used to build the solid cornerstone of our very unique Magic Castle®. On the other hand, our lives would have been a lot easier without Mr. Lipshultz ... or was it Lipshitz? And no, Mr. Lipshultz is NOT a member of our club!

Queen Victoria vs. the Zolotone Monster

After World War II, a popular way of modernizing old houses and buildings was to use a product called Zolotone. This was a cover-all salt and pepper paint guaranteed to disguise architectural blemishes like cracked plaster, peeling ceilings and other reminders of the past. When Tom Glover bought the house, the previous owner had turned it into a rooming house and tried to modernize it by painting the entire interior in one flavor of Zolotone. Yes, they painted the walls and the ceilings. But they also painted the mahogany and oak paneling, the carved wood, even the cut glass windows over the entry and the bronze chandelier in Invisible Irma's room. It looked like someone had set off a Zolotone bomb in the house. Everything was covered with the same kind of paint normally associated with the walls of the rest rooms at bus stations.

As a lover of fine old hardwoods, I determined that our first task in restoring the house would be to strip that paint, and other coats of paint beneath it, to the original wood. For the next several months, Don and I spent our spare time working with paint remover, scrapers and wire brushes. It was worth it every time we exposed a new section of the original wood and craftsmanship.

At that time, I was churning out six half-hour shows a week for *Truth or Consequences*. Between the writers' meetings, production meetings and the show tapings, we only had to be in the studio and our offices four days a week. This left three days for working on the mansion.

As far as I was concerned, Sears, Roebuck and Company sold the best and most economical paint remover at the time and a Sears store was close to our home. We went through two gallons every week. Every Friday I would go into Sears and purchase two gallons of paint remover. This went on Friday after Friday, month after month. The task was endless. After many months I could see the salesman in the paint department was getting curious. One day, he finally asked the question: "Excuse me, Sir. It's really none of my business but every week, like clockwork, you come in and purchase two gallons of paint remover. Do you mind…"

I cut him short. "No problem," I said, "You see, I specialize in removing old paint from wicker chairs. The best way to do this is to dunk the chairs in a huge vat of paint remover and swish them around. The paint remover evaporates at the rate of exactly two gallons a week. So every week, I have to dump in two more gallons of paint remover." The salesman was impressed—I'm not sure if he believed me, but he was certainly impressed!

Millionaire's Mansion for $900 Bucks!

What would $900 buy in 1961? How about a millionaire's mansion? Shortly after we started scraping the paint off the woodwork of the old house, I found another old house. The old mansion stood at the corner of Portland Avenue and Adams Boulevard, 900 West Adams. Today a few traces still remain of what once was Los Angeles' *Millionaire's Row*, one grand home after another stretching from Figueroa Street to Crenshaw Boulevard.

In 1961, the insane destruction derby of these magnificent mansions had just begun. The Waters Mansion was a large three-story Victorian delight. It was built in 1888 by the finest craftsmen of the day. It featured fabulous stained glass windows and room after room of carved oak.

My 1952 MG-TD (named Marmaduke) was trained to come to a screeching halt at the sight of any house surrounded by weeds. Peering through a broken window, I saw water cascading from a ceiling light fixture down a carved stairway and onto the parquet floor of the grand entry hallway. Obviously, the vandals had ripped off the plumbing fixtures for the brass scrap value. Rocks had been thrown through art glass windows that today would have fetched thousands of dollars each. This was a house that clearly needed rescuing. The neighbors knew very little about the ownership of the house. They only knew a bank had foreclosed and the mansion would soon be torn down to make way for an apartment house. Who owned it? Who was the wrecker? Who knew?

Photo by Steve Fritz

I called the Department of Water and Power. After all, it was *their* water that was ruining *my* floor! "I'm sorry, we're not allowed to give out that information," the nice lady whined. I asked to talk to a supervisor and got the same response. "Look, Lady! Your water is gushing out of a broken water main. It is flooding the basement. Kids are using that basement as a play pool. By the time you get an emergency truck out there, innocent kids could be dead! I'm a plumber and I can shut off that water, BUT I have to know who the owner is ... RIGHT NOW!" It worked!

The nice lady gave me the name of the owner of the property and asked me to shut off the water. Actually I had shut off the water at the main shortly after I discovered it but my Academy Award dramatic performance got me the phone number I needed.

When I called the owner, the Golden West Mortgage Company, they gave me the name of their wrecking contractor in San Francisco. It was up to them. The owner of the wrecking company said they planned to tear down the house in two weeks. I said I wanted to buy the building materials, windows, mantels, etc. and remove them prior to the demolition. He said $5,000 would just about cover it. I said I was thinking more in the terms of $500. He said, "No way ... the windows alone are worth a small fortune." I said that unless he wanted to pay for a twenty-four hour guard, at the rate the vandals were going the windows wouldn't be worth ten cents. He countered with $2,500.

"Look, the house is at 900 West Adams. How about $900 cash for anything and everything I can rescue in two weeks?" He laughed and said okay. I had just bought a three-story mansion for nine hundred bucks! I hired a couple of hard-working laborers, rented a truck and started hauling away anything I thought I might be able to use in the Castle. After two weeks, I didn't leave the incoming wrecking crew very much to wreck.

Master Plan

At that time, we had no master plan for the Magic Castle® other than we knew we wanted a bar in the main entry hall. I knew the entrance to the house had to be moved to the east side because my deal with Mr. Glover allowed for the building of a new road that would provide a second access to his Yamashiro Restaurant at the top of the hill. The design of this proposed road raised the level of the hill above the level of the front doors. If our plans for a Magic Castle® worked out, a three-level garage would be built to provide parking for the club. If the Castle didn't work out, the garage was designed to link to another future apartment complex Tom Glover envisioned. Either way, he needed the garage to provide the bridge to the Yamashiro.

My newfound treasure trove of architectural goodies suddenly dictated the *plan*. The grand entrance to the Waters' home was about the right size to replace the bay window on the east side of the building. The paneling from the mansion became the front of the bar, the new reception desk and the paneling in the new reception room. Stained glass windows replaced plain glass ones.

Finding that house at that time was probably the greatest stroke of luck that could have happened. I was able to marry two grand old houses to create the beginning of a magical magic castle.

First Photo

My good friend, Ray Avery, a rare record dealer and expert photographer, captured on film the Lane home before it became the Magic Castle®. He used the photo as the cover of an LP he produced called: "Spooky Sounds."

At the time Ray took the photograph, he had no idea I had anything to do with the property. It was simply an old abandoned, haunted house. The photograph was taken in September of 1961. Note that all the ornamental grillwork between the porch posts and the tower was covered with plywood except for one panel. I removed that one panel to see what was underneath on the first weekend I started working on the house. The next weekend I took down the windscreen on the porch. That means my friend Ray took the photograph the exact week we started working on the restoration. That month I also installed those globe-holding fixtures on top of the four balcony posts. They were originally on the posts surrounding the Waters' mansion.

What Goes Up ...

The rickety, old wooden exterior stairway on the right hand side of the photo brings back a few painful memories. The stairway had been installed as a fire exit from the second floor when the place was a rooming house. It was really ugly and I hated it. It was a major blemish on the face of my new *Castle*.

One day I decided to take it down. We all know the old wheeze about the idiot who saws the limb off the tree while sitting on the limb? Well ... I was having trouble prying the top of the stairway loose from the balcony. To get the right purchase on the crowbar, I positioned myself on the top of the stairway. It worked! One good yank and the stairway came down. Unfortunately, I came down with it. It was a pretty nice ride until we reached the bottom. Although I didn't break any bones, I spent many sessions in orthopedic therapy. I'm still reminded of the event on rainy days. I also learned a valuable lesson on the laws of gravity.

Mimeograph

Remember mimeograph machines? In the pre-copier generation, the mimeograph machine was a miraculous invention that printed copies through the concept of *cutting a stencil*. The stencil was a blue piece of coated fabric. If you scratched the coating, or typed on it, it allowed the ink to go through. The very thick ink was held in a drum that allowed just so much ink to wet the fabric between the stencil and the cylinder. A crank turned the drum. The amazing thing about the earliest mimeograph machines, as well as something they called a typewriter, is they all operated without the use of electricity! You never heard the excuse, "I can't get it out today, my typewriter is down."

Our dad, William Larsen, Sr. was a prolific writer in magic. Long before he bought the Thayer Magic Company, Dad wrote patter and instructions for Thayer. Before starting his own *Genii* Magazine in 1936, he wrote countless articles for *Sphinx* Magazine with his writing partner T. Page Wright. (My middle name is Page, named after Dad's best friend and partner.) Sometimes Dad would get an idea for a manuscript such as "Fifty Tricks for Children." Then he would advertise it in the Thayer ad in *Genii*. If he got enough orders, he would sit down and write the book!

That's where the mimeograph machine comes in. Dad would sit in the patio at Brookledge and type the manuscript directly onto the mimeograph stencil. The ideas would go from his brain, through his fingers to the typewriter keys, to the blue stencil. Dad typed with two fingers at a remarkable speed and seldom had to use the correction fluid. Brother Bill and I got to crank the machine and the whole family would sit around the table and collate the finished manuscript.

It was probably a mimeograph machine that started me in the gag-writing business. A great pal, Harrison "Red" Baker and I decided to put out a manuscript of one-liners when we were still kids in high school. Red wrote funny material and, after all, Dad owned a mimeograph machine! (He also gave us a free ad in *Genii*.) The little book was called Baker and Larsen's "In the Aisles." It sold for a buck and was the first of half a dozen very successful Baker and Larsen joke books.

The mimeo was also a great way to get your fingers inky! Bill's first job at CBS-TV was in the mimeograph department. Later, when he was an executive, he used CBS's facilities to put out the first newsletters, (with their permission, I might add.) Over the next several months, one hundred-fifty friends joined the Academy of Magical Arts. Bill and Irene cranked out the first newsletters and they started promoting the Castle at conventions. Most of our loyal supporters didn't really think we'd make it but they all shared our high hopes for our *Impossible Dream*.

The Academy of Magical Arts

The First Board of Directors

While I was hammering, sawing and falling off stairways, Brother Bill and his fiancée, Irene, were busy promoting the new club via *Genii* Magazine. The first announcement of the Magic Castle® was in the April 1962 issue of *Genii.*

There were five members on the first Board of Directors when the Academy was chartered as a California non-profit organization in 1962. Bill, Jr. was the Chairman of the Board and would remain President until his passing in 1993. The other members were well-known magician George L. Boston; magician/writer F. Michael Shields, who was also working at CBS-TV at the time; Alvin Jensen, the son of Dante, the Magician; and Harry Mendoza, professional magician. About two years later, the owner of Hollywood Magic Company, Louis St. Pierre, replaced George Boston due to his ill health.

It's Magic!

The success of our annual *It's Magic!* show gave us the confidence to explore the idea that there might be enough interest in the art of magic to create a full-time nightclub for magicians.

I remembered the great annual shows that the Pacific Coast Association of Magicians and the Society of American Magicians produced. It was a shame that the "big" shows were now being held at school auditoriums and parks. It seemed like magic in Los Angeles was in the doldrums.

I wanted to bring back the big shows. Lights, scenery, a band in the pit, glamour … all that jazz! In 1956, I was twenty-five years old and, like all twenty-five year olds, I knew everything! I was then the Recording

Secretary of the Society of American Magicians, Assembly 22–which meant I wrote the newsletter. I also went to board meetings. Although they had been making money for their treasury doing an annual show at a small community park theater in Los Angeles, I convinced them to let us produce a first class show for them in a first class theater. The Society of American Magicians would provide the talent and we would guarantee that the treasury would make as much or more than the previous shows.

Oliver Berliner and I produced the first *It's Magic!* in 1956. That first show, actually called *Hocus-Pocus '56,* was staged at the now-torn-down landmark, Carthay Circle Theater. Our premiere show was pretty amazing. TV's Art Baker was emcee. The acts included Frakson, Chop-Chop and Charlene, Phil Bauer, Aubrey & Company, "Magic Lady" Geri Larsen, The Chaudets, Harry Mendoza, and Tenkai & Okinu. They all were classics. Ollie and I were proud of the show. It was an artistic, if not a financial, success. Thanks to Berliner's backing, we paid the S.A.M. but the show lost money.

The next year we moved to the Wilshire Ebell Theatre, once again under the aegis of the S.A.M. This time we offered to produce the show with no guarantee to the S.A.M. The show featured Aubrey & Company, John Calvert, The Chaudets, Leo Irby & Company, Harry Mendoza, James Conley & Company. Art Baker emceed–and, oh yes, Frank "Skipper Frank" Herman joined the guest star, a newcomer on NBC, Ernie Kovacs! Ollie and I loved the show. The audience loved the show … and we lost our money. The S.A.M. decided to go back to magic shows in the park!

"Skipper Frank" was a popular fixture on a local television channel running cartoons for the afternoon young set. He was also a very good magician and ran the Unique Magic Shop in downtown Los Angeles. That year, Frank introduced me to Norman and Shirley Carroll. Norman was the ringmaster of the Ringling Brothers Barnum & Bailey Circus. The Carrolls were also the Ringling Brothers' West Coast publicists.

After our second financial disaster, Ollie Berliner and I were about ready to throw the concept of bringing *big time magic* to Los Angeles into a dumpster. Frank insisted that we meet the Carrolls. When I met

Norman Carroll, he said, "You've got a great show, let me show you how to sell it!" The next year we produced the show and even added a performance. Norman and Shirley did the publicity at absolutely no charge! They wanted to make a point and they certainly did. That year everyone in Los Angeles knew about *It's Magic!* We turned people away.

The Carrolls were singularly responsible for the success of *It's Magic!* They made *It's Magic!* into a "Magic Event." We moved the dates of the shows to October instead of earlier in the year. Why? Because the papers loved to print something "magical" for the Halloween season. We learned the difference between "Calendar" and "Cityside." Once a year the art of magic made the papers and it was because of the inventiveness of Norman and Shirley Carroll.

The publicity over the next five years of *It's Magic!* paved the way for the creation of the Magic Castle®. The Carrolls offered to let the world know about the magical mansion. At that time, Shirley told me two things: "Go for the world. We'll tell people all over the world about the Magic Castle®. It's a fabulous place ... but ... you can't get in ... unless, of course, you know a member!" The second thing she said was, "Milt, I'm a publicist. I am going to make you famous. If you ever start believing any of the publicity I am going to give you, we'll part company."

We started getting clippings from all over the world, many in languages we couldn't even read. And it started paying off. People were calling and asking about this strange place. What was this "Mecca of Magic" in Southern California? The Castle became *the* hard ticket place to go. A visit to Southern California was not complete unless you somehow got into the Magic Castle®. The magic of the Carroll Agency's publicity worked! When Norman died suddenly in 1967, Shirley Carroll carried on the Carroll Agency. She let the entire world know what those crazy Larsen Brothers were up to in the world of magic and other endeavors. Shirley is retired now, but the original Magic Castle® publicity is still working.

Those years of writing for merchandise instead of money paid off. I knew about promoting prizes and I did a good job. Too good. They were very happy with my work in the prize department. Too happy! After a few months of promoting prizes while watching the organization hire and fire a number of new writers I complained to Paul that I only took the job in the prize department to have my foot in the door. Now my foot was getting stepped on by a herd of incoming and outgoing writers. He talked to the show's head writer, Bill Burch, and they came up with a plan. While working in the prize department I could submit acts to Burch. If an act was used on the show I would be paid a fee. This would be a way to prove myself.

As assistant in the prize department I had access to the Edwards Productions warehouse where all the prizes were stored. I knew of a secret treasure hidden there. Just beyond the stacks of cartons of toasters, Amana Radar-ovens, Mixmasters and Kiwi Shoe Grooming Kits, was a stack of fiber cases that only a film buff would recognize.

In today's digital world it's hard to believe that the era of 1956 was pre-video tape. When I first started doing *Truth or Consequences* in 1956 the show was performed live on the west coast and then filmed (with the use of Kinescope directly from the TV monitor) on the east and then, that film had to be flown to the West Coast for a later showing. The Coaxial Cable only ran one way? Those films of TV shows were called "Kinescope." The boxes in the back of the warehouse contained kinescope 16 mm films of the great old night time *Truth or Consequences* show.

I asked George Boston if he would have any problem with my looking at the old kinescopes. George knew I was a film purist with really good equipment so he gave me the okay to take the films home overnight to look at them. Those early shows were pure gold. Actually, pure "Old Gold" since Old Gold Cigarette's was the sponsor at the time. If Snag Werris had taught me anything about gag writing it was the theory of switching a joke. An act that played with a Sergeant and Private could be switched to an act that would play equally well with a Bank President and a new teller. I studied the kinescopes and wrote acts using the concepts the show had used before. My acts were new and fresh but, somehow, they had a guaranteed feeling about them. Bill Burch started buying my acts.

One day I got a call from Paul Edwards. The veteran producer of the show, Ed Bailey, and Bill Burch, the head writer, thought it would be a good idea to put Milt Larsen on the idea-writing staff. It seems they were paying out a lot of money for these outside acts. I was *fired* from the Prize Department and *hired* as an idea man, a real live, full-scale, Writers Guild of America card-carrying writer. *Truth or Consequences* became more than a job. It became a career. Writing the show was a daily challenge and a daily joy. It was an incredible experience that lasted, one way or the other, for about eighteen years.

People would always ask what the writers did on a show like *Truth or Consequences*. We certainly didn't write lines for the contestants and, of course, if we didn't know what the contestants were going to say, how could we write lines for Bob Barker's response? We wrote gags and situations. In the on-camera rehearsal, the writers stood in for the soon-to-be-selected contestants and did what we thought they might do. It was fun. People think of *Truth or Consequences* as a game show. I prefer the term *audience participation*.

Since I grew up in magic, I had no problem devising acts and situations involving people. Bobby Lauher, Jerry Payne and I wrote situations for reunions, hidden camera remote jokes, silly stunts, carry-overs, contests, sketches, songs, heart acts, kid acts … in other words, just about everything under the sun. The only set rule was that it had to be funny.

Ralph Edwards also insisted that the show have impeccable taste. Yes, we threw our fair share of whipped cream pies, crushed cars with wrecking balls and dropped guys in old-fashioned bathing suits into tanks of water but it was always done in a way that never, ever embarrassed a contestant.

Most of today's game shows have one set and no costumes. *Truth or Consequences* dealt in elaborate settings, special comedy props and an array of especially designed costumes. (My wife, Arlene, did the cos-

tumes for most of the syndicated shows on Metromedia but I hardly knew her at the time.)

Brother Bill made a very difficult choice in 1968 when he gave up his job as an executive with CBS-TV to devote his energies to publishing *Genii* Magazine and running the Academy of Magical Arts as President for Life. It was a difficult decision for Bill to make since he had been working for CBS for seventeen years. I made a similar decision in 1964 when I realized that I had created a tiger by the tail called the Magic Castle®. Writing *Truth or Consequences* was the best job anyone could ever hope for. I loved writing so the job never seemed like *work*. The Ralph Edwards organization was a fabulous company and my co-writers were two of my best friends, Bobby Lauher and Jerry Payne.

Being on the writing staff of any show for nine consecutive years was something of a magic trick in itself. I realized, however, that dealing with the day-to-day problems of the Magic Castle® meant that I couldn't give my full attention to my writing job. I went to the greatest boss in the world and told him I felt I had to make a decision. I had come to a fork in the road and I took the direction that led to the Magic Castle®. Ralph understood and found a replacement but he also said I could come back to the fold if things didn't work out. I did go back to my old job a couple of years later when Jerry was sidelined due to a tennis accident and then returned full time when Bobby Lauher died in 1973. Thus my tenure with *Truth or Consequences* lasted nine full years on NBC and nine years on and off with Metromedia Syndication.

John Shrum

As a writer you get to know most of the people that transform your written word onto an on-screen reality. Yet, you really don't get to know them. This was the case with the art director for the show. I had been in countless meetings with John Shrum and admired the way he came up with new scenery and sets six tapings a week. John was quite a character. He was a large, tall man who always dressed impeccably. His trademark was a loud vest and a matching bow tie. He had been an art director at KTLA Television and was on the staff at NBC assigned to *Truth or Consequences* as well as other shows.

I really met John when he designed a set for a sketch we were doing involving a Victorian drawing room. I took one look at the set and realized

I desperately needed someone like John to guide us through the Castle restoration. I complimented John on his set and invited him to join me for a drink after the show. We went over to the Castle and I proudly showed John what I had done. The only room that had any semblance of being finished was the reception room. In addition to the oak paneling I had rescued from the Waters' house and the new front doors, I had decorated the walls with red-flocked wallpaper. During the fifties and early sixties there were dozens of Gay 90's and Roaring Twenties bars and restaurants in Los Angeles. They were all decorated with red-flocked wallpaper. John took one look and uttered one of his favorite expressions: "Tacky!" Then he added, "You really do need my help."

We retired to the unfinished *bar* and had the first of hundreds of Old Fashions that would be consumed over the years. At that time our entire bar stock consisted of a bottle of Early Times for Brother Bill, a bottle of Angostura for that needed dash to make Old Fashions for John and myself, a bottle of scotch for partner Don, and a bottle of gin for Spencer & Jean Clyde Quinn (our special banjo playing effects engineer and his wife, an artist and publicist.) The bar refrigerator held a few cans of beer.

John immediately started designing the Castle. He stenciled the walls as they would have at the turn of the century. He enlisted the talents of his friends at NBC to help. His friends were many and they were some of the finest artists in Hollywood. They were young kids who would later become future department heads at NBC. John asked for nothing in return but he made me promise to keep the red-flocked wallpaper in the reception lobby as a reminder and tribute to my bad taste.

In visiting the Castle today you may notice a case with a sample of that original wallpaper on display. Art director Joe Hoffman redesigned the lobby in 1999 and made sure my promise to John was fulfilled. John Shrum passed away in 1988 at the age of 65. You will find his anecdotes throughout this book. He became one of my best friends and a partner in most of my projects.

Our First Bar

Don Gotschall and I decided we needed a grand old Gay 90's-style bar. After all, the old home was Victorian and what could be more Victorian than a big, solid mahogany, shipped around-the-horn bar?

We found that such bars were not cheap. Even in 1962, a really nice old Brunswick bar cost thousands of dollars. Don heard of a bar that had been in a fire in a saloon in Tonopah, Nevada. We didn't know anything about it other than the bar was somewhere in Tonopah, a little mining town between Goldfield and Nevada City. Don and I, like the Motor Boys of *Pulp Fiction* fame, got up early one morning in quest of our bar. Tonopah was much farther than we anticipated. Don was driving and had apparently slept through a couple of direction signs.

It was almost sundown when we finally reached Tonopah. In 1962, the whole town was about three blocks long. There was one hotel and casino. We walked the street looking for a burned out bar or, for that matter, any kind of bar at all. We found a few but nobody knew what we were talking about. We checked into the hotel and started asking the bartenders and the dealers questions.

We had dinner and decided to begin our search the next day. I had fun and was pretty lucky at a friendly crap table. It was nothing great but for a guy that considers not losing is winning, I did really well. About midnight I decided to turn in. Don seemed to be having a pretty good time impressing some cowgirl at the blackjack table. About five in the morning, Don came into the room and said, "Come on, get up, I've invited the dealers to breakfast." Then he started tossing $100 bills onto the bed! At breakfast, one of the dealers said he knew we had come to Tonopah to buy a bar, but they didn't know it was *their* bar!

We finally found our bar. It turned out to be a few charred remnants behind a saloon. Apparently our information was incorrect. The saloon was saved but the bar had burned to ashes.

Our New Old Bar

We made the Grand Salon bar out of the dining room paneling and the parquet flooring from the Waters' mansion. I had sawed the legs off an antique library table in order to get the well-endowed carved gargoyle look that I associated with Victorian bars. I made the top of the bar back out of porch spindles and plywood. The whole bar looked pretty authentic for a six-stool bar. Actually, the main bar at the Castle is almost the same as it was back in 1962, although it has gotten a little longer over the years.

Slide Show

I told John that I had wanted a big cut-glass mirror or some really great stained glass for the center of the back bar. Then I remembered some old glass stereopticon slides I happened to chance upon. They were hand-tinted *coming attraction* slides for the vaudeville acts that used to play the Los Angeles Hippodrome on Main Street. They dated back from 1916 to the early twenties. The old Hippodrome was torn down in the early fifties but the Main Street lobby remained until a couple of years ago. The second floor housed the legendary Main Street Gym. Before the recent wrecker's ball hit, you could still drive through the fifty-foot long entrance to get to the parking lot that replaced the main theatre. The façade of the original theatre was a joy to behold. Adelphi Theatre, the name before it was changed to the Hippodrome, was carved in terra cotta with theatrical masks that peered around vases and tablets that proclaimed comedy, music and drama.

I became interested in vaudeville while I was still in high school. At that time, the late 40's, the once grand Hippodrome had been reduced to a 24-hour movie *flop-house.* For two bits, a wino could sleep off a bad bottle of Muscatel in a paper sack. I heard the "Hipp" was going to be demolished and figured it was worth twenty-five cents to see it prior to its demise. The doorman was obviously not used to seeing a well-dressed, clean-cut, young kid entering the theatre. "Take any seat but don't sit next to anybody … it ain't safe!" Actually I had timed it to see the theatre during intermission and didn't plan to stay for the movie … I'm allergic to fleas!

At the end of the intermission, I started to leave and the old man was concerned. "Somebody bother you? Don't like the picture?" I assured him I had only come in to take a look at the theatre before it was gone. With this, he told me that he was over ninety years old. He had started in show business as a magician and took me on a real tour of the old showplace. It was amazing. There were animals' cages and a huge swimming pool under the stage. There was even a little movie theatre under the main auditorium, where the parents could park their kids while the vaudeville show was on. It was a huge place with gilded boxes and balconies rising to the gods, ornamented with thousands of Mr. Edison's new fangled light bulbs framed in plaster rosettes.

Just before I left, I tripped over a box in the projection room. It was filled with those wonderful glass slides. I asked if I could buy them. "You want 'em, kid? They're yours!" So, those priceless slides on the back bar cost me a quarter—and they are worth every penny.

The slides under the glass on the Irma side of the bar were part of a missionary's temperance lecture. I found them in a junk store. They were from the 1920's but the messages are still pretty topical.

Jay Ose

Bill and I realized that a club devoted to magic should have great magic entertainment. We started casting for our first Resident Magician. We wanted someone who could entertain with fine close-up magic, something kind of rare in California back in 1961. Most of the really well known performers worked out of New York and Chicago: Dai Vernon, Johnny Platt, and Al Goshman? They were all still back in the east. After all, that's where the work was. Our choice was Jay Ose. The name is Scandinavian and Jay pronounced it "O-See."

We met Jay through the magician comedy writers "Snag" Werris and Lou Derman. Snag Werris was my comedy-writing mentor and had been the writer for some of America's top comics on radio and TV. At the time of the opening of the Castle, he was writing for Jackie Gleason. Lou Derman loved magic and was one of Hollywood's top writers. Among the shows he created and wrote were *December Bride* and *Mister Ed.*

Jay Ose had led a very hard life. He was a gambler, drifter and an alcoholic. When he handled a deck of cards, it was with the experience of a man who knew the tools of his trade. In Jay's earlier life, those tools were not used to entertain. He was a man who had hit the skids and he might have checked out of this world long before 1967 if it hadn't been for the Salvation Army.

Jay was a Captain in the Salvation Army when Snag and Lou suggested he might be the right man for the job at the Magic Castle®. We balked at first. After all, the idea of a former alcoholic working in a club with a bar might provide too much temptation for the average person. But then we met Jay. Through the Army, he had found God and had found a new life. He swore he would never touch a drop for the rest of his life and he kept that oath. Every time I make a donation to the Salvation Army I think of the fact that, without them, we might have lost Jay and, without Jay, the Castle might not have been so successful.

Bill, Jay and I made a deal. In return for a room at the Castle, and the promise of a job as a permanent magician when the club opened, Jay agreed to live at the Castle as a sort of night watchman. At the time, we all thought the Castle would open early in 1962. Jay lived alone in the creaky old house for over a year in what is now the Dante dining room. At that time, it was a very plain room with little more than a bed, a little electric heater, a hot plate and a can opener. But Jay never complained. He had a private bathroom with plumbing that worked about half the time. It wasn't exactly the Ritz and with the construction going on it must have been like living in a war zone.

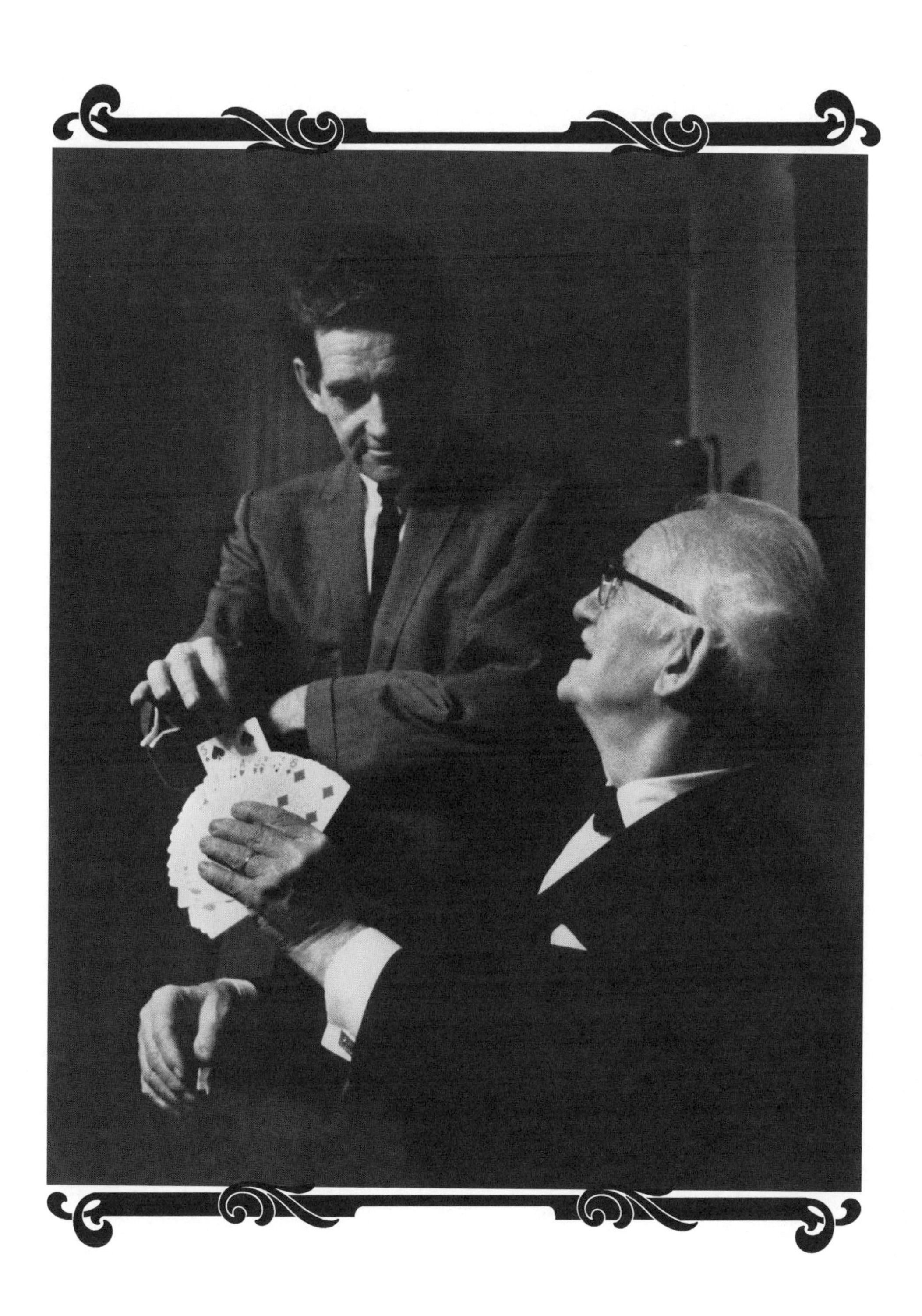

During the day and night buzz saws and hammers created the only magical sounds heard in the Castle. Upstairs, Jay had his own little club. Playing a game called *Klobiache* you would find Harry Blackstone, Sr., Benny "Tin Ear Benny" Roth, "Canada Jack" Walsh, Snag Werris and, of course, Lou Derman and his brother Bill. One day I told Jay I needed to make a new door in his wall. He said he was going out anyway and the mess wouldn't bother him. A little later, my chain saw ate through the plaster and wood lath and I heard a yell. I found a plaster-dusted Jay Ose, who had returned without telling me and had decided to move his bed out of the way. He thought I was talking about an opening in the opposite wall!

When the Castle finally opened we knew we had made the right choice in selecting Jay as our Resident Magician. In addition to being a brilliant card manipulator, he was always charming and made each and very guest feel like they wanted to become a member of this very special club for magicians. He looked like a con man and had the class of a king. Over the first five years of the Castle, Jay was certainly the key element in making it a hit. The biggest names in show business brought their friends to see this remarkable little man with his delightful gift of gab. People from all walks of life wanted to be a part of this unique magical experience. His magic was flawless and there is no doubt that his personality was one of the reasons for the early success of the Magic Castle®.

In the very early days, Jay would keep a plywood tabletop hidden behind the love seat. On very slow nights he would haul out the plywood top, throw it on the floor in Irma's room and tap dance on it! He was as delightful a dancer as he was our consummate magician.

"Mr. Junk"

John Shrum introduced me to Ernest Evans, owner of Scavenger's Paradise. The license plate on his truck read: "Mr. Junk." He was a delightful, witty and charming man who had the appearance of Ernest Hemmingway. Ernie had a rare talent for finding and saving architectural treasures from houses and buildings that were being torn down. His main clients were the film studios but he also sold to the public, when the spirit moved him.

I used to call him "the man with the velvet crowbar." Ernie was like the dentist that didn't *pull* teeth ... he *liberated* them. One day Ernie taught me one of his great secrets. A great old mansion on Barkley Square (Santa Monica Freeway and Western Avenue) was being torn down for a parking lot. The home was the largest residence ever built in Los Angeles up to that time. The woodwork was fabulous but the wrecker assigned to the demolition project had ruined a great deal of the built-in cabinetry by trying to *pull* it from the house. It was sad to see piles of polished but splintered mahogany and pieces of once beautiful paneling scattered around the grounds. Ernie was given a few days to pick up whatever he could salvage from the house.

Ernie wanted to save a beautiful built-in mahogany and cut-crystal bookcase. You could see where the former wrecker had tried to pry it from the building and had damaged it in his failure. Ernie simply went around to the exterior wall. He tore off the siding with an ax and affixed a chain around the exposed wall studs. The other end of the chain was attached to his trusty old stake truck. He got in the truck and revved up the engine. In a few moments, the wall was on the ground and the beautiful piece of woodwork had been liberated from the house. It was one helluva trick!

Some good advice: Don't try the above method of rescuing woodwork unless you seriously want to tear down the whole house! Ernie passed on those secrets to his son, Rick, who still runs Scavenger's Paradise on Satsuma Street in North Hollywood.

Another son, Glenn, is one of Hollywood's top special effects specialists and has been a major help in many of our Castle projects.

Even in 1962 carpeting was very expensive, especially commercial grade. Ernie came to the rescue with a load of carpeting from an old hotel on Bunker Hill. The carpeting was old but in great shape and all it really needed was a good cleaning and de-lousing. The best part was that it was free. We just needed to buy some new padding. John Shrum called a friend who did all the carpeting on the set at NBC. He became "Carpet George" and he installed our newfound treasure in our first four rooms.

Bob Lauher, Jerry Payne and I were the three writers on *Truth or Consequences*. What are they doing in a story about our early carpeting? Jerry Payne had just bought a house in the Hollywood Hills that had been owned by the legendary comedian Eddie Cantor. Cantor had probably plugged some carpet company on the radio or TV show because his entire house was wall-to-wall in red and gold theatre carpeting. Jerry gave us the carpeting and once again Carpet George installed it when we opened new rooms at the Castle.

Second Hand Milt

In the early days of the Castle almost everything we had was bought used or at auctions. It was simply a matter of economics. Restaurant and bar equipment is much cheaper after the first place that spends a fortune for it goes broke. Often we would redesign a room just because we bought something that wouldn't fit in the original plan. We always had to face the fact that the wonderful Lane home was built as a residence. John Shrum would say how much he would give to design a Magic Castle® in a Safeway store, a free-span building with no bearing walls or posts. Alas, we had an old house with many bearing walls and many posts. On the other hand, that is what makes the Castle rather charming. It's obvious that we have dealt with what we had and perhaps that's part of the secret of the Castle's success.

Permits, Nice People & Good Luck

As we got closer to opening, we started learning about little things like permits and licenses. It seems the city, state and federal governments have certain rules you need to follow. Most of them were pretty easy. After all, we weren't in business yet. One of the first things we had to do was to change the power service. When renovation began, the house was powered by a fifty-ampere service. Remember those old glass fuses that people used to put pennies in? That meant no conduits. It is called knob and tube wiring, state of the art electricity at the last turn-of-the-century.

You have to remember that when the Lane home was built in 1908, electricity was something fairly new. At that time, people thought fifty amps would power the world! To show their faith in the incandescent lamp, the Lane's had their house plumbed for both gas and electricity. We put in a new electrical service—two hundred amps—that should hold us for years!

Obviously, dealing with the city led to having an electrical permit and, as anyone who has ever built anything knows, that led to the question of all building permits. I toddled down to City Hall with the idea of walking out with a building permit. Those crazy people actually wanted to see a plan of what we contemplated. We had a bar? Had we consulted the health department yet? Did we have our plumbing permits? Were we actually going to change the occupancy from a private residence to a club?

In those days, the Los Angeles Building and Safety Department occupied one big room at the City Hall. All the inspectors seemed to know each other and it probably broke the monotony of their day to have a complete non-builder, comedy writer, magician in their midst. They patiently explained that all projects need plans that had to be approved by all agencies before work could proceed. No, plans drawn on the backs of cocktail napkins wouldn't do–not even plans from the NBC scenic artists would work … They wanted real live, genuine plans. This was getting to be more work than fun. I wanted to hammer and saw and create Castles–after we finished, it would be easy to give them a plan.

The city was firm. I could keep scraping paint but no hammering and sawing without a plan. Those nice guys at the plan desk were getting a little impatient. Tom Glover introduced me to a great guy by the name of Colonel William Butz. He was a semi-retired structural engineer and, under Tom's urging, agreed to take on our project. He drew up some preliminary plans and we went down to the City Hall together. When we arrived, Colonel Butz threw his plans on the desk and said for all to hear: "Don't look at 'em, son, just stamp 'em!" The clerk laughed, looked at the plans, stamped them with their approval and told us to get out of their office and move on to the next agency. I didn't know that Colonel Butz had been the head of the building and safety department for years before he retired. He had a great reputation and the staff loved him. Tom Glover did know all the right people in the world.

At one time after we opened, a Hollywood health inspector came in and started giving us a really bad time. After making us sweat a bit, he introduced himself as Dr. Donald Hardenbrook, one of our most enthusiastic magician members. He was a great help to us in our early years.

Chapter Two

Happy New Year 1963

Opening night

The Magic Castle® opened on January 2, 1963, because we somehow knew we wouldn't be ready for a New Year's Eve party. We barely got open on the 2nd. Because of the holidays our liquor license had been detained. Until the Alcoholic Beverage Control office in Sacramento approves the license you can't buy liquor from a wholesale distributor—and you couldn't sell the stuff even if you could buy it! In those pre-fax days, they would *wire* the approval and number as soon as they had it.

One of our founding members, Snag Werris, the noted comedy writer, also owned a liquor store. He graciously volunteered to drive to the distributor to pick up our first order of booze as soon as the license was approved. Our scheduled opening was 6 p.m. Snag arrived with a carload of liquor at 5 p.m. He always had a way of saving the day!

Johnny Carson did a very hilarious sketch in which he talked to the Jolly Green Giant. This involved making huge green giant legs. After the show, John Shrum couldn't resist the temptation. John knew that Snag liked to stay up very late and get up very late. This gave John the chance to send the NBC truck to deliver the two huge green feet and a few dozen watermelon-sized kernels of corn to Snag's house. When Snag came out of his house that morning, he found a neighborhood full of gawking on-lookers. The Jolly Green Giant stood on Snag's lawn until our own Harry Coles volunteered to move them to his Rancho Amigos Hospital where, as far as I know, the kids may still be enjoying them.

Our first bartender was an Irish pixie by the name of Joe Sullivan. Joe was well known to the CBS-TV crowd, having worked in various watering holes around the studio. He was one of those old-time bartenders who always tended bar wearing a high silk hat. Joe used to tell the Castle regulars that it was good luck to toss silver coins over the spindles that form the crown on the back bar. He said someday someone would pull out the bar and find a treasure in coins.

When I expanded the bar to the full length of the room a few years later, I figured all those coins would be mine ... I'd be rich! We pulled out the original back bar and found only three dimes and a nickel. It seems Joe had figured out a neat system of retrieving the coins on a regular basis! Joe was a great character and now serves the Great Mixologist in the Sky.

Spencer Quinn, Irma & Open Sesame

The late Spencer Quinn and I built the original Invisible Irma. It was very primitive! I got the idea from a description of The Aeolian Harp in the 1897 book *Magic*, by Albert A. Hopkins. It seems the harp had been presented at the Colombian Exposition in Chicago in 1890. A harp was displayed in a chamber and spectators were amazed that it would respond to their requests as if an invisible player was present. I had worked my way through high school repairing mechanical musical instruments and my good friend Spencer, an excellent musician, was fascinated with the concept. We won't tell you how Irma works today. We prefer to think of her as a full-time ghost who simply sits down and plays the piano every night, to the delight of her friends. When the Castle opened, we felt the proper place for the piano was in the original Music Room—that was the round room in the tower that is now the Close-up Gallery.

The secret of the first Irma was simple. A live piano player operated a remote keyboard that opened valves on a player grand piano. Spencer punched leather valves out of an old belt and we ran a network of eighty-eight aluminum tubes from the piano to the remote operator in the cloakroom behind the reception room. It was a crazy idea, but it worked!

Spencer made his fame as one of the best banjo players in the business. He knew an out-of-work piano player by the name of Bill Groom. Bill had been with all the big bands and had a tremendous repertoire. We met him that first night and told him about a strange and wonderful old ghost by the name of Irma who might want to play during his breaks. We thought the guests could enjoy our tuxedoed pianist for an hour and then have fun with the Irma gag for five or ten minutes. From the night we opened, we found our guests loved our invisible piano player and really didn't care about seeing Bill Groom … except maybe for John Carradine.

As it turned out, this was great for Bill. Apparently he couldn't hold down a cocktail piano job because he would get angry with the guests when they requested songs. This way he could sit in the back room and yell at the guests who couldn't hear him. It was a perfect job for Bill who was Irma's best friend until his passing many years later.

Because of the length of tubing between the cloakroom and the piano, there was quite a delay between the moment of hitting the note and hearing it. Bill would hear a request on earphones and then have to take the earphones off to play the song silently on his keyboard. One day Bill was at his keyboard on the Castle's first really, rainy day. No one had given much thought to the fact that the cloakroom, after all, was a place to hang coats. Bill found himself being rained on by a mass of dripping raincoats. That night, we decided we had to re-invent Irma. Of course, later we found that Irma really was a ghost so we didn't need that mechanical fakery.

Spencer engineered our first "Open Sesame" entrance door. When I was a kid, I built secret doors that would hide closets and back rooms at the family home, Brookledge. I was greatly influenced by those wonderful old Abbott & Costello and Bob Hope "Ghost" films. We wanted a gimmick when the guests entered the Castle and a secret door was obviously the way to go. I filled the original bookcase with real books. It was hinged, on rollers and replaced an existing door. Spencer invented a system of ropes and pulleys to make the door open on command. When a guest said the magic words, Spencer would step on a lever under the desk and the door would mechanically swing open. It was no problem since Spencer weighed in like a football linebacker. It tested fine but, on opening night, our lightweight receptionist stepped on the lever and went straight up in the air. Spencer had to provide the ballast for the entire evening.

Spencer's wife, Jean Clyde Mason Quinn was a professional designer and artist. She had designed our first promotional brochure and had never waited a table before in her life. She was suddenly proclaimed *official cocktail waitress*. Mark Wilson stood on Irma's grand piano and floated Nani. It was a photo that would make Newsweek Magazine. Brother Bill and fiancée Irene, Don Gotschall, John Shrum, my then fiancée Barbara Logan and I welcomed everyone while the incomparable Jay Ose, Resident Magician, entertained the amazed guests for the first time. We somehow made it through that night and the Magic Castle® was off and running.

Immediate Success

Not really! W.C. Fields once uttered a great line in his monologue "The Day I Drank a Glass of Water." He said, "Those were the days—I hope they never come again!" Considering our advertising was all word of mouth and Bill's constant plugging in *Genii* Magazine, our patrons were slow in finding us.

There were nights we would run old movies and nights when Spencer Quinn would accompany a remote operated nickelodeon piano on the veranda with his banjo while Jay Ose tap danced, much to the dismay of the neighbors. They put up with a lot. At one time, I had a Mills Violano mechanical violin in the dining room. It was an amazing machine, regarded in its time as one of the most remarkable inventions of the day. The problem was it worked on some sort of static electricity. That was fine except all the TV sets in the vicinity went bonkers every time the machine was played. I quietly traded it for a 1927 Alvis Motor Car that I later traded for the grandfather clock on the Castle grand staircase landing, before the neighbors figured out who the culprit was.

At the time we opened the Castle I was engaged to a wonderful lady, Barbara Stuckey, professionally known as Barbara Logan. Barbara was a brilliant and gregarious person who was well suited to her career in publicity and marketing. Barbara and I were both very career minded. We really didn't want to settle down to marriage at the time. Had the Castle not opened that year we would have gotten married and had a child. We decided to wait, a decision I have regretted all my life. In 1966 she was the publicity director of Phil Rose of California, a major sportswear firm. One trip to Japan the plane carrying all the executives from the firm rammed into Mt. Fiji. There were no survivors. In just a few minutes time, my future changed. I always felt very guilty about the fact that, if we had made different decisions, she might not have been on that plane.

Management

Eleanor St. Germain was the original one-lady-office tour de force of the Magic Castle®. When we opened the Castle in 1963, our first manager was Don Culp. Don was driving a Good Humor Ice Cream truck at that time so we figured he knew something about the food business. We needed someone to handle the office affairs and Don knew that Eleanor, a widow with two sons, needed a part time job. I knew Eleanor as one of the world's greatest Al Jolson fans, which meant she was okay in my book.

George Bardossas, a young Greek kid we engaged as our first janitor, replaced Don Culp. Don left us and became an executive with Executive Car Leasing. George never picked up a mop because we needed a bar waiter more than we needed a janitor. George had been working in restaurants and knew the bar business. We knew Don wasn't perfect for the job when Bill asked him to get some goodies to nibble on at the cocktail hour and Don bought dozens of sugar cookies. Cookies and Manhattans? Never!

George and Eleanor were an amazing pair of workers. Bill was still at CBS and I was still at NBC. Bill was running the affairs of the club from his office and I was building the Castle on my days off. But George and Eleanor were there; daily fending off the myriad of problems that faced our growing business.

When my fiancée, Barbara Logan died Eleanor was there with care and understanding. She became much more than a secretary. She became a very large part of my life. No matter what the daily disaster was, Eleanor would plant her feet squarely on the ground and defend the fort. When I opened the Mayfair Music Hall in 1973, I stole Eleanor from the Castle to run the office at the Mayfair. When we opened the Variety Arts Center in 1977, I stole Eleanor from the Mayfair to run the office at the VAC. She was an amazing human being.

After her sons, Bernie and Phillip, became adults, she moved to Greenwich Village to pursue her lifelong dream of becoming a playwright. She wrote a play about Lorenz Hart that would knock your socks off but couldn't get it off the ground due to a rights problem with the Hart Estate. She has since passed away but we have great memories of a very special lady.

Three Rooms, Magic & Six Stool Bar

When the Castle opened we had only a six-stool bar in the main lounge. I was the first chef! Well, not really. I was still writing *Truth or Consequences* and found myself with one of the prizes, a Black Angus Rotisserie–a little portable electric broiler. People kept asking for some kind of food so I came up with *Steak Diablo*. It was, simply, a small tenderloin steak from the local Safeway market broiled on the Black Angus rotisserie and sliced in cubes. It was served *pupu* style with toothpicks and my very own special secret sauce, the secret recipe for which I can't remember. Originally, we were going to produce it magically from a chafing pan but that idea only got as far as the first few press photo ops.

Albert Goshman

One day I was fixing the Blank Angus special when a rather disheveled young man came in and offered some good advice. "Throw the thing away and use the stove!" He explained he was a baker from Brooklyn who knew the value of using professional equipment. This was my first meeting with the legendary "Baker, who is a Faker" Albert Goshman. I remember thinking Brother Bill had finally flipped out. Here was a guy in a dirty tee shirt that Bill had hired as one of the first to lecture for our magician members. He was a doughnut maker from Brooklyn, no less!

Then I saw Albert perform. He was a man with charisma, charm, and an act! He had a real live, well thought-out, beginning, middle and end act! Soon everyone was looking under the salt shaker and saying, "please." Albert Goshman became one of the Castle's most popular magicians.

He has played throughout the world and brought an offbeat dignity to the art of magic. One of Al's best routines involved the use of *sponge balls*. These little balls were expensive and he complained about the poor quality of most of the sponge balls on the market. So he figured out a way to make his own. Then he started selling them. He had no competition in a very lucrative market. Al knew how to make money, and how to save it. He often came to the financial rescue of the kid he met working on that Black Angus Rotisserie and the club that we like to call the Magic Castle®. He was always there when we needed him (at a high rate of interest).

Leo Behnke & Dai Vernon

The first lecturer at the Magic Castle® for the Academy of Magical Arts was Leo Behnke. Leo was an excellent and inventive close-up performer and became our second Resident Magician. The first lecture was booked seven weeks after we opened. It was held in the unfinished *living room* on the second floor. We had just painted the room and some of the members had to sit on stacks of lumber and packing crates instead of chairs.

Dai Vernon came to lecture at the Castle in March of 1964. We let him stay with Jay in his room for a week or two. Dai found a new home at the Castle and stayed for the next three and a half decades. It seems like the magicians who came out west to lecture or perform at the Castle usually used only half of their two-way ticket. The Castle became the new home for people like Johnny Platt, Don Lawton, Al Goshman, Senator Crandall and many, many others.

The Larsen Annex

Most of the early lectures were held at Brookledge since we really didn't have space at the Castle until later. Those lectures were very popular since Bill always liked to open his personal bar for his guests. Bill and Irene were married November 25, 1963. Irene was also from the world of magic, having been married to John Daniel, one of the art's finest illusionists and a builder of magical apparatus. John had met Irene when he was in the Army stationed in Germany. She became his principal assistant in his spectacular Allakazam magical production. Bill had been previously married and had a daughter, Wendy. Irene and John had a son, Dante. The Larsen family grew to include Heidi and Erika, daughters of Bill and Irene.

Harry Blackstone

Harry Blackstone, Sr., one of the greatest names in magic, lived in an apartment two blocks down the street from the Magic Castle®. Oliver Berliner and I presented Harry on the 1959 Edition of *It's Magic!* at the Pasadena Civic Auditorium. It was a very unionized house and the musician union killed us with a twenty-one-piece orchestra in the pit. We had more stagehands than we had acts. Harry was in his late seventies but he was still great. He was, however, a little slow and the show was running late. I remember sitting in the back row of the large auditorium with Ollie looking at our watches. We knew that if the show finished by 11 p.m., we would break even. If the show went one minute past eleven, we would be in for a major loss.

He was still going strong as the clock ticked past eleven and into overtime. Let's just say it was worth every penny for us to see the old master at work and to have been the producers of one of Blackstone, Sr.'s last full-stage performances. Needless to say, we were back at the non-union Wilshire Ebell Theatre for the next dozen, and more, years.

One of our first international publicity breaks came, thanks to Shirley Carroll, with a Globe News Syndicate spread that featured the Magic Castle® and appeared in papers all over the world. Most of the papers carried a cover photo of Harry Blackstone floating a lady in front of the Magic Castle®. The lady was Brother Bill's new bride Irene Larsen. Irene was one of the best, and most beautiful, magic assistants in the business.

There was nothing magical about the stunt. Spencer Quinn and I rigged a beam that projected out of a dormer window in the attic. Through block and tackle pulleys and some piano wires, we hauled Irene up past the second floor while the photographer shot away to get that one picture we needed. The photo was great and Blackstone and Irene graced the covers of magazines and newspapers everywhere. If you look closely at the photo, you will see our own Spencer Quinn, with his hand raised strangely in the air. Was it an odd affection from this burly banjo player? No, it's just that someone had to hang on to an invisible fish line to keep Irene from revolving in the breeze.

Blackstone—
The Second Story Man

In 1962 we announced the idea of the Magic Castle®. At that time Harry Blackstone, Sr. was elderly and not in good health. He seemed like he was about ready to check out. We showed him the old house before we opened and he could see the same vision we saw. We always believed the anticipation of the club gave Harry a new incentive to live. The old man became amazingly young again.

One day, he wanted to show some of his friends what we were doing on the hill and I agreed to meet him. He and his friends arrived and no one was there. The house was locked. Our show taping had run late. By the time I got there, Harry was sitting at our mock-up close-up table doing card tricks for the ladies. When I asked how he had gotten in he explained he had found a ladder and simply climbed up to the second story open window and had crawled in! So much for old men checking out!

Harry loved the club and held forth almost nightly at the Castle. When we enclosed the original porch we called it the Blackstone Room in his honor. Harry passed away November 16, 1965 but his memory, and the memory of his son, Harry Blackstone Jr., live on at the Magic Castle® in the Blackstone Room.

John Schuyler

Our first host was John Schuyler. Jay Ose dubbed him "Tuxedo John." His full name was John Brevoort Schuyler III. With a name like that he should have had a stable of polo ponies. John was blonde, young and charming, six foot something with a flashing smile that would light up the room. John was our official host and greeter but he also loved to tinker with technical gimmicks and electronics. This led to a very successful career as a film technician.

One night John and I were working on the room that was then my office in the tower. The tower windows had a commanding pre-high-rise view of Hollywood. We had been talking about Invisible Irma and testing a number of the *spirits*. John suddenly noticed that the flag was still flying over the Hollywood Roosevelt Hotel. Now in the sixties, the flag was supposed to be lowered at sundown. (Today you may leave your flag up as long as it is lighted. Unless, of course, some radical wants to burn the flag, in which case, it is wise to lower it.)

John thought something should be done. He called the night manager of the hotel and told him that the flag was still up. Then, he went on to pretend that he was a salesman for the Constitution Steam Flagpole Company. The pitch was hilarious. Did the hotel have steam? Of course, all hotels had steam. He explained that the patented automatic flag-raising flagpole worked entirely on steam—the only way to go. It was a sidesplitting performance for an audience of one.

John Schuyler Quake Story

Tuxedo John cut an Adonis-kind of image. He had absolutely no problem dating very lovely ladies. When the big Sylmar quake hit in 1971, John was living in an apartment next door to the Magic Castle®. The Larsen ancestral home in the Wilshire district shook like hell but suffered little damage. At that time, Brother Bill and his family lived in the main house on the property and my bachelor digs were in the theater building at the rear of the estate. After checking on the family, Bill suggested that one of us should go to the Castle.

Thinking we were probably some of the only survivors, I drove up Highland Avenue, past dozens of fallen brick chimneys and broken windows to see what, if anything, was left of the Magic Castle®. I had visions of our priceless art glass dome scattered all over the floor, chandeliers and rare stained glass scattered throughout the house. Even worse, hundreds of bottles of booze lost forever! To my surprise, the Castle had absolutely no damage. Everything was still standing. It was real magic!

The chimneys had also fallen on the apartments next door but the neighbors gathered outside were talking about only one thing. Apparently Tuxedo John and his lady friend had been making early morning waves on his new waterbed. At the first shock of the quake, the pair shocked the natives by running out of the apartment buck-naked. By the time I heard the story, the bystanders had embroidered it to include the graphic description of our host's continuing his amorous activity with his partner on the front lawn. In fact, some witnesses said they were doing it smack in the middle of Franklin Avenue.

When It Rains

On really rainy days at the Castle you can usually count on a few leaks in the roof. After all, the original house is almost a century old. I always claim the buckets under the leaks are only another way of creating an authentic Victorian atmosphere. Our landlords, the Glovers, have spent thousands of dollars re-roofing the Castle but those leaks always appear like magic. Luckily it doesn't rain that much in Southern California.

Insurance ala Levinson

If you look at the old photos of the Castle, you'll notice a grand veranda surrounded the corner tower. When the road to the top of the hill was completed in 1964, we enclosed the front porch, which is now the *Blackstone Room* and made a covered area out of the veranda so people waiting to see the close-up shows could keep out of the rain. Before that, the porch was a great place to sit and inhale the carbon monoxide exhaust of the arriving cars. When Ernie Evans found a bunch of matched rocking chairs, we put them on the porch and started serving mint juleps during the summer. Bill Bixby and Ray Walston, who were then starring in *My Favorite Martian* on TV, often held rocking chair races on the veranda to the delight of the guests.

Since the road to the Castle wasn't finished, our parking attendant (singular) would park cars along the edge of the hill. One night insurance mogul Member Harold Levinson drove up in his big, new Cadillac and came in to enjoy the club. Levinson was a very funny man and a major force with the Masquers Club down the street. He was very wealthy and very generous. The attendant parked his car on the edge of the hill—the usual place of honor for expensive cars. A little later in the evening, Member Dave Powers drove up in his old station wagon. Dave was then an Assistant Director at CBS-TV who later became one of TV's top variety and sit-com directors.

The attendant was busy parking another car so Dave left his car in the front of the Castle. Somehow, the brake didn't hold and the car rolled down the hill. It stopped when it hit Hal's Cadillac. The Cadillac rolled over the curb but luckily stopped when it hit a large water pipe halfway down the hill. The water pipe broke, creating a geyser of water that, of course, started undermining the dirt beneath the Cadillac.

The Veranda Gang thought this was a great show and called me out to take a look at the disastrous scene. I took one look at the mess and went back into the club to find Hal Levinson. He was calmly sitting at the bar and said someone had already told him about the accident. He asked me to keep him informed and went on chatting with his friends. By now, the Veranda Gang was applauding the efforts of a frantic tow truck driver. His truck had slid over the edge of the hill in a sea of mud. A second tow truck had been called and Hal's car was now sandwiched between the first tow truck and a tree.

I told Hal about the latest catastrophe and the unruffled insurance man asked if he could use the phone. He called his wife at home and said: "Dear, why don't you meet me at the Castle for a nightcap and, oh ... (without missing a beat), by the way ... bring the Lincoln!"

Bill Bixby

Bill Bixby was already a member of the club when he was cast in the series *The Magician.* Bill loved magic and was perfect for the role. He played a James Bondish-type of magician headquartered in a club very much like the Magic Castle®. The show might have been a huge success except for the fact that, in the earliest segments, Bill wasn't allowed to do much magic. He was seen driving his gas-gobbling car into the cargo bay of his gas-gobbling private jet. The shows were aired in time for the huge gas shortage crisis in the late seventies.

The show looked like it was filmed at the Magic Castle® but they only used an exterior establishing shot. All the sets were on the Paramount lot. Nevertheless, we used to get a lot of mail addressed to Bill Bixby at the Magic Castle®. Fans assumed his office was up in the tower where my offices were in the early days.

Gambling

In the first days of the new close-up room, the area where people line up now was an open porch. One day we were visited by a couple of officers from the Vice Squad of the LAPD. It seems they had gotten a complaint that flagrant gambling was going on at night at the old mansion on the side of the hill. Apparently, two old ladies from the neighborhood came up and peeked through our windows to discover this major den of card sharks and dice dealers. After being royally entertained by Resident Magician Jay Ose while Leo Behnke did his famous dice stacking magic, the officers left peacefully and said they might arrest the old ladies on Peeping Tom charges.

Irma Room Switch for Close-Up Room

It didn't take too long for us to figure out that the round room we were using for Irma would be a better Close-up Room and vice-versa. First, we built a real gallery in the round room where the magician could sit and perform for about four spectators. The rest of the audience stood on tiers very much like an operating gallery. Later, we would go to the theatre seating we have today. Jay Ose, Al Goshman, Johnny Platt, Leo Behnke, Charlie Miller, Dai Vernon and others delighted audiences in this room.

Ernie & Irma

Ernie provided tons of priceless junk that we used to *restore* the old mansion. One day I got a call from Ernie. He said, "Come on over and pick up your frame." He explained that he had found a grand old gold frame that he thought would look nice somewhere in the Castle.

I jumped in my pickup truck and found Ernie sitting in his favorite rocking chair outside of his store. Next to him was a dirty old frame. It was so dirty that you could not see the portrait behind the glass. I agreed it was a nice frame and wiped some of the dirt away, exposing a charming Victorian pastel of a naked child in a chair. When I asked him what he wanted for it he said: "You owe me another dinner." We seldom dealt in real money. I put the frame in the back of the pickup and started to leave.

Another pickup double parked abreast of me and blocked my way. It was Harry Goodman, a well-known art dealer on La Cienega Boulevard. Harry jumped out yelling, "Are you buying or selling?" When I said I had just bought the picture, he said he'd give me twice what I paid for it. Figuring this was a chance for Ernie to make some real genuine money, I asked if he wanted to sell it to Harry. Ernie just sat in his rocker and said: "You can't afford it, Harry. Besides, Milt needs it for the Magic Castle®!"

That evening I polished up the frame and the pastel and showed it to John Shrum. Immediately, he went into the Irma Room and told me to take down a poster that was hanging over the fireplace. I replaced it with the picture of the kid in the chair. To this day, we still claim it is a picture of Invisible Irma when she was a child. Who knows, maybe it is!

Milt, the Carpenter

My usual costume for working around the Castle is work boots or tennis shoes, Levi's or shorts, tee shirts or sweatshirts. It's not exactly the image of a club founder or executive. I was working in front of the Castle when a guy pulled up and asked to talk to someone in charge. I asked if I could help and he rather brusquely informed me that he really wanted to talk to a manager or the owner. I put down my tools and asked him to wait. I went around to the kitchen door and had a quick cup of coffee. Then I walked out to the lobby, opened the front door and told him I was the owner and we weren't buying whatever he was selling. He went away.

Then there was the time I was hammering and sawing when the fire inspector came. He said he had been in a few nights before and was concerned because there was only one exit door in the new close-up theatre. I said it wasn't really a theatre and it did have two doors. There was one from the lobby and one from the main lounge. He very nicely pointed out that, in case of fire, the fire department didn't really approve of exits that don't go directly outside. Going back into a burning building didn't make sense.

I agreed with him and pointed out that a door could be cut in the wall that would go outside. I asked him to wait and shortly returned with a fire ax. Then I asked him where he wanted the door. He pointed at a spot in the wall and I started chopping. Apparently, I made the inspector's day. For years, the department talked about the crazy magician that instantly complied with the fire department's request.

The Carpenter Act

The third floor was sealed off during the first few years. We simply didn't need the space. Then we started using the servants' rooms as an office and a library. The late John Shrum came up with a great plan for turning the unfinished area into a new library, a grand tower office and

more storage space. Diners would sometimes wonder about the *ghosts* hammering in the attic.

We used to be closed on Mondays. I was up on the third floor, hammering, sawing and thinking up hilarious stunts, when I got a call in the early afternoon. The caller asked if I wanted anything special in the way of technical help for my act that night. Act? What act?! It seems, several months before I had promised to do an act for the Comedy Cabaret night at the Society of American Magicians meeting. The call was from the stage manager and they wanted me to be at the Trouper's Auditorium on La Brea at 7 p.m. Well, a promise is a promise. I said I would be there.

At that time, I really didn't do an act. I'd always haul out my six-card repeat and serpent silk and a few other props and do the same tricks and patter that Dad used to do. I had promised a "comedy act!" It was now about 3 p.m. No time to go home and put on the old tuxedo or find the props that I only used once in a while. I was wearing boots, Levi's, a dirty T-shirt and a carpenter's nail apron.

I ran down to the shop and quickly made a breakaway table that I would chop up while trying to cut a rope. I found a picture frame that I thought might get a cheap laugh from the magicians by doing a parody on a glass penetration. I sawed up a gas pipe and painted it to look like a cane, which wouldn't quite vanish and made a few other gags. I threw this junk in the back of my pickup truck and arrived right on time for the SAM meeting.

That was the way my "Carpenter Act" was born. The audience had never seen a magician go berserk before their very eyes. They laughed. Thank God, they laughed! (PS I still treasure the trophy I won that night as the "Best Comedy Act of the Year." It's a gold-plated ear of corn.)

Milt's Portrait

John Shrum had a marvelous, if somewhat warped, sense of humor. It's hard to miss my life-sized portrait that hangs over the grand stairway. It's not a big ego thing, although I must admit, it was my idea to hang a huge mirror at the top of the stairs so you can view the painting as you ascend or descend. The painting is a fine piece of art. The artist was Gerald Mouser. At the time it was done, Jerry was making a living as a scenic painter at NBC-TV. Later, he became well known as a fine and very expensive artist doing portraits commissioned by Robinson's.

The idea behind the painting should be credited to photographer Warren Samuels. Warren had seen me working around the Castle in my usual shorts, tee shirt and carpenter's apron. Why not white tie with tails, with an apron and a martini? Yes, Warren took the picture before I dressed that way for my comedy carpenter act. Our late, great friend and associate, John Shrum, had heard me comment that "success is when you have a bigger painting than Alexander Pantages." I was referring to the life-size painting of Mr. Pantages that used to hang over the mammoth lobby of the Hollywood Pantages Theater.

On my birthday, April 9th, an NBC truck arrived with a huge crate from John Shrum. The instructions read that I couldn't open the crate until the champagne corks started popping later in the evening. I had no idea what it was ... but I did notice one thing. The heavy plywood crate was held together by screws. Not your usual box nails, but hundreds of old-fashioned slot-type wood screws! It was long before Makita battery drills were in existence.

The party started and John handed me the first present. The package contained a nice new slot screwdriver. My job was obvious. While others quaffed their drinks, I sweated over the task of removing the screws, one by one. Just as I was nearing the end, Shrum flipped his necktie over his shoulder (a habit which indicated he was about to do or say something funny.) He grabbed the screwdriver and very easily pried the back of the crate open. The back appeared to be screwed together but those screws were only screw heads! It was held together by a few small nails. What a great, rich joke! I never knew what John paid Gerry Mouser for the painting, but that crate had to have cost Johnny Carson a fortune.

Gene Fowler's Chair

Gene Fowler was a living legend. A Hollywood fixture in the literary world, Gene was a novelist, biographer, poet, screen writer and friends with some of the most famous, talented writers of the 20's. My personal favorite novel is *Minutes of the Last Meeting* which recalls the days of the "Bundy Drive Group" which included the likes of W.C. Fields, John Barrymore, Jack LaRue, John Carradine, John Decker and Sadakichi Hartmann. It's a wonderful tribute to Fowler's writing skills.

I sat in Gene's green leather swivel chair as I wrote the lunch menu stories. The family gave us the chair and other memorabilia to be included in a Gene Fowler exhibit which may someday find a home in a new variety arts museum. In the meantime, I get to sit in his chair. Maybe there is such a thing as *ass-to-ass transmission*. Whether there is or not I feel I'm a better writer when I'm sitting where a truly great writer once sat.

Gene's son, Will Fowler, wrote an excellent biography of his dad called *The Young Man From Denver*. Will followed in his father's footsteps and became a very well known journalist. His own autobiography is called: *The Second Handshake*. He said people would often meet him at parties with a limp handshake. Then the introduction would be: "Will Fowler… Gene Fowler's son." At which point he would get a rather firm handshake. His other son, the late Gene Fowler, Jr. used to be a fixture at the Magic Castle® bar along with his cronies from the film-editing world, most notably the late Cotton Warburton. Gene Fowler's hat collection, hats left in his writing den by stars and famous people of Hollywood, is displayed in cases above the Hello Dolly bar area.

Tablecloth Yanking For Fun and Profit

Somewhere along my life's path I picked up the talent to do the old party gag of whisking a tablecloth out from a table loaded with dishes and glassware. The gag has gotten me a lot of work, usually doubling for a film star in a motion picture. There is no great trick to table cloth yanking. You simply have to know what you are doing and you have to have an amazing amount of confidence in the outcome.

Photo by Virginia Hunter

Many years ago I got a call from Bill Asher's office about doing the bit on the old *Bewitched* show. I went to his office, cleared his desk and set up a small demonstration. One yank … no problem. He booked me on the spot after asking if I could do it with a fully set dining table. When the day of the shoot came the prop guys showed me the table and also hundreds of pieces of dishware and glassware. Obviously they assumed there would be a lot of sweeping up to do. I sat on the set for three days dressed in Paul Lynde's suit. Each day they said they didn't want to take the time for the bit. Finally they braced themselves for the great moment. They assured me I could do as many takes as necessary to get the shot. I asked them to roll the cameras on the first attempt. After all, it might work in rehearsal and never work again.

It seemed like every crew member on the lot crowded the set to watch the disaster take place. The table was set and I did the yank. It was perfect on the first take. There was total silence for a long pause until the *clear* bell rang. At the bell the catwalks and stage shook with the applause of the cast and crew. I was the hero of the day and have collected residuals on that show for many years. I was Gomez' back on *The Addams Family Values* and Everett Rupurt's back on *Dinston Check's In.* The strangest gig I performed was doubling for the puppet, *Skeeter,* in an episode for the TV series *Cousin Skeeter.* Try yanking a tablecloth while standing in a hole in the stage wearing furry animal paw gloves. That one took more than one take!

Bedknobs and Broomsticks

Richard M. Sherman is half of the Sherman Brothers songwriting team. Dick, and his brother, Robert B. have two Academy Awards and eight nominations to their credit. Although they are mainly known for their work with Walt Disney, which includes *Mary Poppins* and *It's a Small World After All*, their list of hits is incredible. Dick has also entertained Magic Castle audiences with his lectures on magic and music. Our friendship goes back about fifty years. When the Sherman brothers were assigned the task of writing the score for Disney's

Bedknobs and Broomsticks they got the idea of writing a song for British actor David Tomlinson, who played the part of a magical professor and phony conman. The song was *With a Flair* and Dick and Bob convinced the Producer that Tomlinson could do some wacky magic roughly based on gags from my own gentleman carpenter act.

I got the job as magic consultant and spent seven weeks working on the film. Director Bob Stevenson thought it would be fun if I played a bit part in the sequence. I royally enjoyed playing a deadpan stooge as Tomlinson dumped a hatful of broken eggs on my head. Although I had been a longtime member of both the Screen Actor's Guild and the American Federation of Radio and TV Artists, everything I had even done up to this point was on the little TV screen.

When the picture was released I was thrilled to see myself on a giant cinemascope theater screen. That was at the trade preview of the film. Naturally I told all my friends about my big screen debut. When the picture was released at Radio City Music Hall in New York City it had to be drastically shortened to fit into their stage show schedule. Twenty minutes was cut from the movie including the entire *With a Flair* musical number. Seven weeks of work and my entire motion picture debut ended up on the cutting room floor. Thanks to good friend and Disney film editor, Cotton Warburton, there was one fleeting glimpse of me in the crowd but in reality my credits were on longer that I was!

Twenty-five years later in 1997, thanks to the efforts of Disney's Manager of Library Restoration, Scott MacQueen, the film was restored and re-released as a special 25th Anniversary Special Edition.

Richard Sherman and I have written a hundred or so comedy songs over the years under the banner of *Smash Flops* and a couple of stage musicals *Charlie Sent Me* and *Little Old Broadway.* It has been a long and wonderful friendship.

Sunset Boulevard

I was always on the lookout for building materials to use for the Castle. The film *Sunset Boulevard* with Bill Holden and Gloria Swanson (1950, Paramount) was not filmed on Sunset Boulevard. The grand old mansion was actually on Wilshire Boulevard at Crenshaw. It was a huge home and it stood vacant for many years before and after *Sunset Boulevard* was filmed there. The house was torn down to make room for the Tidewater Oil Building.

Just before the demolition there was a sale of building materials from the house. Naturally, I was there to see what could be scavenged. Because of the *Sunset Boulevard* connection, the sale drew a number of gawkers. I wandered through the mansion and found myself in the library. The room had magnificent paneling and one of those “walk right in and get yourself warm” fireplaces right out of *Citizen Cane*.

I like to look for the traditional secret room or secret panel in those old houses. They all had them and you kind of knew where to look. I walked around the room tapping on some of the polished mahogany panels. I didn’t realize it but I was being observed by some of the folks. I found a return in the paneling by a window seat and noticed the head of a tiny nail. Now we all know a nail head would never, ever show in a perfectly paneled room like this one. I took a ball point pen from my pocket and pressed on the nail head.

“Sproooong!” As I suspected, this was the latch to a secret panel. A small door sprung open, disclosing a cubicle. The door hid the contents from the others in the room that were now trying to hide their curiosities. The only thing inside was a very pretty, little wooden chest. I peeked inside. It was empty. Now, I knew the chest was empty, but all those curious people watching didn’t know. I couldn’t resist.

I quickly closed the chest, shut the secret panel and furtively left the room to find the wrecking company foreman. Finding him, I quickly explained the whole scenario and the fact that the gawkers were dying of curiosity. The guy played it like he was straight out of drama school.

I opened the box and he reacted to the emptiness as if it was King Tut's Tomb. I whispered that I was parked on the side street and it would be funny if we jumped in his truck and sped off. He could drop me off around the block and the looky-loos would never know what was in the empty box.

The foreman had a great sense of humor and we played the game. He gave me the little box and even drove to the back of the property so the people wouldn't see him come back. When I left, there were about three-dozen people standing outside comparing notes. It was a fun day!

The Second Floor

A House is not a Restaurant

When architects Alison and Alison designed the Lane home in the early 20th century, they had no idea a bunch of magicians would show up half a century later to turn the lovely residence into a club with theaters, bars and full dining facilities. The kitchen was on the main floor where it should have been because the dining room was adjacent to it. We put our dining rooms on the second floor and, for the first many years, our waiters kept healthy running up and down a flight of stairs to deliver dinner. There were two small bathrooms on the second floor so naturally that's where we put the service bars. Brilliant design? Nope. We simply put sinks where the original designers put the plumbing!

John Shrum always said he needed to be a magician to make a house, with all the rooms too small and in the wrong place, into a practical working restaurant. He claimed I handed him my *impossible dream* and it became his impossible designing nightmare.

On the other hand, the Castle's intimacy and not-quite-perfect charm is probably one of the keys to the club's success. The fact that we never knew exactly what we were doing made the whole project exciting and fun.

Ernie's Dome

We're not quite sure where the magnificent art glass dome in the main dining room came from. When we found the dome, it had been stored for a couple of years on the roof of Ernie's Scavenger's Paradise barn. Ernie told me one day that he got it out of a solarium of an old mansion at 3rd and Burlington in Los Angeles. He thought someone named Van Stuyvesant owned it. That's close enough for our kind of history!

The upstairs living room in the old house was very plain. If we were going to make it into a grand old Victorian dining room, it needed a lot of help. Our Guru of Grandness, John Shrum, remembered that Ernie had stored a large dome on his roof. I went out to look at it and there it was, a masterpiece art glass in an iron frame covered with years of dirt and bird badness. (It's amazing how accurate those flying devils can be when they have an interesting target.) I asked Ernie if he would part with it. He said he liked the idea of sitting under the dome and having dinner at the Castle. He figured he had about one hundred-fifty dollars invested in the dome and that was his asking price! Even in 1963, art glass was bringing in pretty big prices. This was Ernie's way of saying, "It's a gift!"

Shrum gave me a plan of where the dome should be installed. The plan was a square drawn in the middle of the back of a cocktail napkin. The next problem was how to install it. The obvious answer was to remove the roof of the Castle, hire a big crane and a flat bed truck, bring in a bunch of workmen and get the job done. It all seemed very complicated and very expensive. Then I made an interesting discovery. The entire frame was put together with bolts. Each pie shaped section could be removed and dealt with separately. I carefully measured the frame and engineered the hole that would have to be cut in the ceiling.

For the next few days the big question was "What happened to Milt?" There was a lot of hammering and sawing on the third floor attic. What was the mad carpenter up to?

It took about a week of framing. Only John Shrum and I knew a giant hole was about to appear in the dining room ceiling. That hot summer Saturday I took my pickup truck, a screw driver and wrench set, a six pack of beer and a bottle of sun tan lotion to the roof of Ernie's barn. Later that day, the dome was dismantled and in the back of the truck.

Jay Ose used to live in the bedroom that is now the Dante Room. Sunday he was playing cards with his buddies, Lou Derman, Dai Vernon and Kuda Bux. They thought the San Francisco earthquake was doing an encore when I dropped the original ceiling—one hundred forty-four square feet of half-century old lath and plaster and dust. By the end of the day, the job was done.

I hauled each panel up three flights of stairs and bolted the frame together. It was worth the trouble. It looked as if the ceiling had fallen and a rare treasure had been unearthed. I called Shrum, who came over with Ernie and we had the first dinner under the new dome. John brought the pizza and I made the Old Fashions.

After the dining room had been open for a few years or so, we decided it needed a little more pizzazz! To dress up the room we placed twenty-foot tall shutters from the Norma Talmadge building on Sunset strip on their side and used them as vintage paneling. John suggested that we stick mirrors on each panel. It would make the room look bigger and reflect the glories of our grand dome. It was a great idea so I measured one of the panels. Then I counted the panels on the top row and ordered the custom cut antique gold-veined glass. When the glass came, I learned another great lesson in craftsmanship. “Measure twice, cut once.” They should have added, “Measure everything!” I had measured the one and only panel that was about one inch smaller than all the rest. To this day, you may cast your eyes on that mistake of thirty some odd years ago. The top row of mirrors is too narrow and doesn’t match the second row. Please don’t tell your friends. It’s terribly embarrassing.

Food For Thought

Our first real chef was Harry Phillips. We hired Harry when we started serving dinners in the first dining room on the 2nd floor ten months after we opened the doors. Harry was an excellent old-time grill chef who was semi-retired and was the father of an early member, Thalia Phillips. The food was good but strictly steak and chops.

Harry did a great job considering we were using the original residential kitchen and non-commercial equipment. I found an old galvanized iron hood in a junkyard and a blower that was woefully inadequate for the job.

Harry was Greek and spent a great deal of his time chasing the waiters around the kitchen with a meat cleaver. The waiters had to run up the back stairway to deliver the food. One of those waiters was a young man by the name of David Aguirre.

David Aguirre

David Aguirre has been with us forever! Well, maybe not forever. The Magic Castle® has been open since 1963 and David has only been with us since 1964! David is our affable and super efficient maitre d’hôte most evenings and Friday lunch. In 1995, he made the local papers in a very interesting article about his restoration of the last remnant of the old Black Foxe Military Institute, a Mediterranean Revival-style building that once housed the schools founder and headmaster. If memory serves, I believe Harry Blackstone, Jr. went to Black Foxe. Since we lived in the Hancock Park area, I knew the area well as a kid. They had their own polo field that butted up against the exclusive Wilshire Country Club's golf course. After the school closed in 1968, the acreage became the site for a large condominium project.

The house David bought was abandoned and considered a major blight on the, otherwise, stylish upscale neighborhood. David had rehabilitated two other houses in the Hollywood area and had won the accolades of his neighbors by rescuing the property from hookers and drug dealers. David got the property recognized as a Los Angeles Cultural Heritage monument. From the head restorer of Cultural Heritage Monument #195 to the head restorer of Monument #618, thanks for a great long run at the Castle!

Victorian Festalboard

Salad bars were not in vogue in the sixties. I think the Castle had to be one of the first salad bars in the country. One of our favorite restaurants and watering holes was the old Cock n' Bull on the Sunset strip. They were the inventors of the *Moscow Mule* and Bill and I had many of those copper mugs to show our loyalty to the Cock n' Bull bar. Their food service procedure was the waitresses served the salad and then you served yourself from a prime rib buffet. We simply reversed the idea. We let the people help themselves to the salad and appetizers and the butler served the entrée.

Later we stole something from another favorite Sunset strip bistro. We robbed the Frascatti Inn of a Danish waiter, Klaus Riisbro. I wanted to make the salad bar more interesting so we added items reminiscent of a Scandinavian *smorgasbord*. Klaus hired Gerard and Bengt, two chefs that had worked for Ken Hansen at the legendary Scandia, and the "Victorian Festalboard" was born.

I coined the word *Festalboard* and invented the story about Queen Victoria's visit to King Oskar and her commissioning the Palace chefs to recreate a British version of an elaborate array of gourmet delights. Real historians will recall that Queen Victoria never set foot away from the British Isles, but no one has ever questioned my story. It's interesting to note that a number of restaurants have since used the name Festalboard in their menus. They say, "imitation is the sincerest form of flattery." We are flattered!

When Bengt and Gerard left us to open their own restaurant they said they had a fine chef to take over the reigns of the food service. We had an appointment to meet their choice for a new chef one afternoon. On that day, a very jolly man came in and introduced himself. His name was Howard Prindle and his most recent credit was that of Executive Chef at the Officers Club, Edwards Air Force Base. We asked, why had he left his former employer? Howard responded that he had lost his temper and had purposely dumped a plate of one of his favorite dishes in the lap of an obnoxious three-star general. Well, at least he was honest.

We hired him on the spot. Later that day, another man came in and announced that he had been sent over by our Chefs Bengt and Gerard. We had hired the wrong chef! Howard said he just happened to drop by because he heard we were a club that served food—he was in the neighborhood. He had never heard of the Magic Castle® or ever met our two Scandia chefs!

Howard Prindle did a fine job running the food service and setting up the restaurant at our Mayfair Music Hall enterprise in Santa Monica. He was with us for many years before turning his efforts into creating food for TV and film shoots. Howard's life was filled with peaks and valleys but he always was a very charming and talented man. Knowing him was something of an experience. Howard had some personal problems that led to his dismissal from the Castle staff. After losing him, our salad chef, Louis Perez took over the Executive Chef position. Louis was a great guy but he really wasn't a creative chef. The food at the Castle was always good but out of step with the better dining rooms of the eighties. Members will remember that our menu didn't change for many years and many would blanch at the thought of another serving of stuffed trout. The Castle started getting the reputation of "a great place to go, but try to have dinner someplace else." Unfortunately that reputation was very hard to shake.

Several years later, when Louis voluntarily retired, we put together a great staff and added a few new employees. What we needed was someone to train these talented people and create a new approach to our menus. We found a brilliant young world-class chef to do the job who worked closely with management and our food service staff to make the Castle a wonderful dining experience as well as an entertainment adventure.

Dining at the Castle

Art Ryon and the Times

The late Art Ryon, of the Los Angeles Times, wrote the very popular restaurant column "Roundabout L.A." which was later taken over by member Robert Dwan's wife, Lois Dwan. Art was highly respected and, if Art Ryon said a place was good, it was sensational! One night, one of our members brought him in. Bill and I met him and showed him around the Castle. He had dinner and left.

To our surprise, his next Roundabout column was devoted totally to the Magic Castle®. He raved about the food and the service. He loved the magic and the ambiance. He explained that non-magicians could also join this fabulous club and gave his readers the proper phone numbers and statistics. All of a sudden, the people of Los Angeles knew there was a very special club for magicians: the "Magic Castle®." It was our first big break.

Art became a big supporter of the Castle until his death a few years later. At one time, I mentioned how much that early review had meant to the Castle and to us personally. He admitted the review was a little voracious but he wanted to help our struggling club. Why? It seems that Art Ryon started his career as a reporter in Pasadena. One attorney had taken the time to help that cub reporter scoop others in a very important case. That attorney was our dad, William Larsen, Sr. Art had never forgotten the favor and said, "thank you" to dad by helping his sons make their dream Castle come true.

Numero Uno Chili

Howard Prindle was the man responsible for the recipe for our *Numero Uno* chili. He had been making his favorite chili recipe for our employees and as a late night snack. The chili was never on the dinner menu. One day Ruth Dosti of the L.A. Times happened to drop in with a member. We didn't realize who she was or that she was doing a survey of Los Angeles' restaurants. The next thing we knew, the Magic Castle's chili was listed as number one on the L.A. Times list of the town's ten best chilis. It was a total surprise to us. She pointed out that the best chili in town wasn't available to the general public. You could only get it at the Magic Castle®, a private club. (For your information, the much-touted Chasen's famous chili was number three!)

Friday Lunch

In the mid-sixties we started serving lunch Monday through Friday. It was not successful. Later members kept asking about lunch so we came up with the idea of having lunch on Friday only. On December 6, 1968 the waiters discovered we were out of lunch menus. They had been ordered but not yet delivered from the printer.

Instant printing had just become popular so I hastily knocked off a temporary menu and ran down the street to our local Postal Instant Press. I had fun with the menu and added a few of the names of members who regularly attended the Friday lunch sessions.

When the fancy printed menus finally arrived, members said they missed my little weekly *Gazette*. The brand new fancy menus went on the shelf and I started writing my fun little column. For the first ten years I wrote stories about my old friend Professor Harry Hockmann. Many of those stories can be found in our book "Hockmann, the Great Exposes Himself!" (Brookledge Publishing ©1998) Then I started writing stories and anecdotes about the building of the Magic Castle® and the book you are now reading is the result of about twenty years of those weekly columns.

Cobb Salad

The manager of the Vine Street Brown Derby restaurant was Bob Cobb, whose name is now legendary because of his *Cobb Salad*. Cobb originated the salad because he always liked a little snack at closing time. He simply took leftover lettuce, turkey, bacon, avocado, etc. and chopped it all up. In those days, proper salads were never, ever chopped ... it was against the Epicurean rulebook. Cobb would share some of his salad with his closing-time cronies and, before long, the waiters were being asked for one of Cobb's salads.

Today you will find the Cobb salad on menus throughout the world. The dish varies tremendously as chefs add their own touches. The Magic Castle® Cobb Salad that we serve for our Friday lunches is prepared exactly the way Bob Cobb made it over half a century ago. Why? We have a lovely member by the name of Peggy Cobb, Bob's daughter, who gave us his original recipe and supervised its preparation. Peggy said Bob's description of the salad was that it had to be "mooshie."

Cocktail Hour

In the first few years of the Magic Castle®, we had an interesting little group of cronies who used to enjoy the cocktail hour. They would come in about five, after work, and we'd toss them out for lack of coat and tie at 7 p.m. They included such wonderful characters as Cotton Warburton, the football all-star and Gene Fowler, Jr., the son of the legendary novelist. Both were then top film editors. We also had a little clique from the Peterson Publishing Company, which included top magazine writer W.R.C. Sheddenhelm.

Many people think the Castle was an instant success. It wasn't. We had the usual growing pains of starting a new business. We had no investors and no capital. There was always more money going out than there was coming in. Luckily, Brother Bill and Don Gotschall were still gainfully employed by CBS and I was still writing for Ralph Edwards, but the early economic seas were turbulent.

When we needed money for air conditioning, Bill put out one of his very personal newsletters asking members to contribute to the fund. They responded and we were able to put in the necessary twenty thousand dollars' worth of equipment. Members still thought the odds of our making it were slim, but they had faith. I put my writer's paycheck in the barrel every week to help pay the bills.

My original partner, Don Gotschall had put in the original twenty thousand to cover the liquor license and he was sharing the losses. Love had entered his life and he decided to get married. The realities of married life against pumping money into an impossible dream forced Don into a decision he hated to make. Golar Enterprises would have to become just Lar Enterprises or Larsen Enterprises in the future.

I tried to find someone who would buy Don's half of the partnership. There were no takers. Dreams are nice, but twenty thousand dollars is a whole lot of money, especially then! Don is still a good friend and Life Member. He is now retired and living in Florida. He always visits the Castle when he's in town. We sometimes are forced to make decisions we'd rather not. After all, Bobby Lauher and I turned down the opportunity to write a pilot for a TV show called *Laugh-In* in favor of a guaranteed sixteen half-hour TV shows called *Malibu U.* starring Ricky Nelson. One never knows.

Toby Palmieri

One day I was sitting at the bar with W.R.C. Sheddenhelm quaffing my usual vermouth-less martini. He commented that I wasn't my usual cheerful self. I confessed that I had a major financial problem. I had to come up with five thousand dollars by 10 a.m. the next morning or the Castle could be history. W.R.C. thought a moment and then said: "Why don't you ask Toby?"

Victor "Toby" Palmieri was quite a character. He belonged to that cocktail hour gang and would drop in almost nightly. He was short and portly, many times wore khaki shorts and sported a beard that needed a tamer. He looked like a guy you'd think twice about hiring for your next safari. He also had a rather awkward habit of belching and would occasionally rock over on the bar stool and release excess gases in other ways. He was the last person in the world you would ask for a sawbuck, much less a five thousand dollar loan. But, what the hell—W.R.C. pushed me in Toby's direction.

I explained my dilemma and he laughed. He said there was no way on earth that he could come up with five thousand! Then he added, "by 10 a.m. the next day." He went on to explain that his bank didn't open until 10 a.m.—it would be at least 10:15 before he could loan me five thousand dollars. The next morning, I met Toby at the bank and he handed me the money. It saved the day.

For some time after that members would sometimes question our being a little lenient with the *slob at the end of the bar*. They never knew he was a knight in shining armor and had rescued the Castle in a moment of disaster. Toby was a young man when he died. In his will, he left twelve hundred dollars to be spent for a wake in his honor in the pub of the Magic Castle®. It was to be an open bar hosted by the late Toby and the will specified that the party would last until the last drop of twelve hundred dollars' worth of booze was consumed.

Regular Regulars

In the early days of the Castle, on slow nights, Spencer Quinn moved in a mechanical upright piano nickelodeon, which was controlled by some buttons on his banjo while Jay Ose would tap dance on an extra plywood table top he kept handy.

All that was fun but the real magic of the Castle was always the magic and the wonderful aura of love of the art by all those who entered its doors. It was never unusual to find Harry Blackstone, Sr. entertaining with card tricks in the Blackstone Room. Carazini would perform at the

drop of a hat on the grand stairway landing. Richard Zimmerman could be found sitting on the floor in front of the fireplace producing unlikely objects like bricks. "Torchy" Towner would occasionally entertain our guests with a bar-side flame-throwing illusion.

Maury Leaf

Maury Leaf was another Castle regular who absolutely loved performing and audiences loved watching him. Maury was a pixie-ish man with snow-white hair. He was a character straight out of a Dickens toy shoppe. As a collector of old 78 r.p.m. personality recordings, I was probably one of the few people in the Castle that knew Maury had been a vaudeville monologist in the twenties who had recorded some of his monologues for the Columbia Gramophone Company. He was a master dialectician. His *John Smeet Meets Pocolhontal* is a classic. But Maury's past accomplishments as a comic were long ago.

Maury had become a major technician and inventor in the motion picture business. In retirement, he loved magic and his magical toys were far advanced from anything most magicians knew about. To magicians at the Castle, watching Maury Leaf was like watching a latter-day Robert Houdin. His greatest audience-pleaser was his version of the classic "Snake in the Basket" trick. Maury had a card selected and the snake found the card. Just like every other snake in the basket? No way. Maury's "Snk" had a personality and an attitude. The "Snk" was actually Maury's voice doing some of the accents he used in vaudeville. The way the "Snk" moved and reacted fooled the most diehard magicians. Maury's widow, Kay Leaf, let me have boxes and boxes of gears, wheels, springs, motors and goodies that Maury had in his shop. I still thank him for saving that one little part that I find I need.

TED
SALTER
1986

Friday Night Lou

Jay Ose dubbed him "Friday Night Lou." That didn't mean Lou Derman didn't come in on other nights, but the late show Friday was his favorite spot. Lou was very much part of the formation of the club and later served on the Board of Directors. He was one of television's most successful writers, probably best known as creator and writer of the top-rated series about a talking horse, *Mr. Ed.* Lou loved to perform and he was hilarious. His wife would actually time his show with a stopwatch to see how many laughs a minute he got. The laugh count was always staggering. For many years Lou Derman wrote the *Knights of the Magic Castle®* column for *Genii* Magazine.

Ted Salter

The caricatures that flooded the walls of places like Sardi's, The Brown Derby, The Friars Club, Masquers Club, Lamb's Club created a wonderful atmosphere. Ted Salter was one of our charter members who had a commercial art service just a few blocks from the Castle. Ted had been a successful music hall magician and puppeteer in England before moving to the United States. Once in a while Ted would dust off the old puppet acts with his wife, Eileen, and it was a delightful show.

One day Ted came in with a caricature of Jay Ose and asked if we wanted to display it. We started talking and I asked if he would be interested in doing a few more. That was the beginning of the Castle's remarkable collection of hundreds of caricatures spanning a period of thirty years by this very talented artist. He donated his work to the Castle and constantly refused to commercialize on his efforts. Ted retired in 1995 and moved to Hillsborough, N.C. He left a major legacy to magic through his talent.

Harry Coles

Harry was member #R104, which means he joined about a year before the Castle opened. In those days the Associate Members could join for a $25 entrance fee and the Magician (Regular) Memberships went for $35 (that pricing reversed once the club opened). Harry was an ex-prizefighter and most of the "tricks" he knew involved dodging punches. He figured the Brothers Larsen needed support for their crazy dream so he kicked in the extra ten bucks and became a *Regular* member. Since then he has hung around enough magicians to easily qualify but, in those early days... a buck was a buck! Harry was a dear friend and a great supporter of the club. He was a fixture in the lobby every Christmas at our members kid's party playing the part of Santa Claus. Since Harry was black he always kidded about the fact that he was from the *South Pole*.

Celebrities

The Magic Castle® has always had its share of celebrities. Many stars are big magic enthusiasts and a number of them, like Milton Berle, Harry Anderson and Johnny Carson, are excellent magicians. Stars like the club. Our *no cameras, no autographs* rules give them the privacy of their own private club.

One of my favorite celebrity stories goes back many years. One night, Jack Denton, a local TV personality who portrayed F.D.R. in *Annie*, dropped in. Jack was a member and loved the Castle. People recognized him as "Oh, there's ... what'sisname, you know, the guy on TV!" Next Bob Barker came in. At that time, Bob was the very popular star of *Truth or Consequences* on NBC. Bob has always been a very supportive member of the club. Everyone recognized Bob. Then member Karl Malden entered with two guests for dinner. They were Hume Cronyn and Jessica Tandy.

Gracie

Just as the members and guests were getting used to this star-studded evening, Cary Grant came in with Tony Curtis. Cary was a member of the Board of Directors and came in quite often. His radiant personality never failed to light up the room. People would always whisper, "My God, that's Cary Grant!" Tony, of course, had played Harry Houdini on the screen. They had popped in for a quick drink and a show. What a night!

The stars left in exactly the reverse order. Cary and Tony said goodnight; Karl, Hume and Jessica left next. Bob went home. It was late and Jack Denton and I were talking at the bar. Someone came up to him and said: "Aren't you the guy on TV? Would you sign his napkin for my daughter?" Someone else piped up with: "Gee, Jack. It must be nice to be a star again!"

Cary Grant

I first met Cary Grant when I was a kid working for George Boston at Abbott's Magic store on Hollywood Boulevard. George took off for a few hours and asked me to mind the store. My first and only customer came in and cheerfully asked what was new. I demonstrated a new trick and he acted as though he had never seen it before. He wanted two of them. This enthusiastic customer bought at least two of everything I showed him. He stayed about an hour and had a great time chatting with his teenage salesman. By the time he left, the bill was over two hundred dollars, a huge sum in the late forties.

When George came back he asked if I had sold anything. I showed him the multi-paged sales slip. George was amazed when I told him all the sales were to one sole customer. Did I know who it was? Sure, George, everyone knows Cary Grant! What a day!

Cary became a member of the Castle in 1966 and graciously offered to fill a vacancy on the Board of Directors when the President asked him if he would. Because of his charm and dignity, members and guests always respected his privacy. He was the super star of films and an amazing man.

One day, Cary was meeting some guests at the Castle, who were a bit late. Cary was obviously concerned. We assured him that the receptionist would call as soon as they arrived, but he became more and more worried that they were lost. At one point, he decided to wait for his lost guests at the door. His guests still didn't show up which resulted in other guests arriving to find a brand new Magic Castle® *doorman*. As people came in, Cary held the door and greeted them: "Hello, my name is Cary Grant and I do hope you will enjoy your visit to the Magic Castle®." Then he would do the whole routine about the Open Sesame owl. People who were coming in were really impressed by our new "Cary Grant look-a-like."

Opportunity Knocking

One night, Cary introduced me to his guests. They were Kirk Kerkorian and a fellow who owned the Frontenac Hotel in Miami and the El Morocco nightclub in New York. Cary said we really should start a Castle in New York and his friend would be interested in the project. I told them I didn't really know what we were doing in Hollywood, much less New York. Maybe later, but not right now. Before Cary left that night he reminded me that his friends were serious and, quote: "Opportunity was knocking." I still said we weren't ready for that giant step and nothing more was said about it.

Another night, Cary was sitting at the Mezzanine bar and said something about leaving the next day for New York. I said I was thinking about making a trip to New York soon. He said: "Come along, there's plenty of room." The next morning, his secretary called to ask if I knew where the plane was. It was right next to Frank Sinatra's jet at the private airport across from LAX. I asked, "When does the flight leave?" His secretary said, "Whenever Mr. Grant gets there, but you should be there around 10 a.m. ... if that's convenient." She explained that all I had to do was drive up to the gate and toot my horn twice to make the automatic gate open.

At that time, I was driving my 1952-MG, Marmaduke, and a pickup truck. I decided I'd take Marmaduke for this very special occasion. You can bet I was the first one there, about an hour early! I drove up to the gate and realized the horn on my MG didn't work. (In sleepy California, we're not big on horn honking.) I spent the next five or ten minutes doing vocal horn imitations for an audience of one gate microphone box. Finally, someone came up behind me, honked twice and the gate opened. (I still have that MG and the horn still doesn't work!)

That afternoon I was having a hot dog with Cary on the Faberge private jet to New York. The plane's steward had explained that they had a full compliment of entrees, drinks and champagne and caviar but Cary preferred Coney Island hot dogs. While we were flying along, I commented on the jet. He said that they were very nice and matter-of-factly suggested that Bill and I should get one. Regarding the Gulfstream II we were flying, Cary said he really preferred his DC3 that he still owned. He said he liked to occasionally take the controls and also the old plane had a large bedroom with a double bed where he could relax and read a good book.

The Gulfstream II was appointed like a Victorian private railroad car. There was a beautiful young lady on the flight who was doing a story on Cary. She looked a great deal like Grace Kelly and was quite charming. At one point, she took a cigarette out of her purse and held it between her fingers, obviously expecting the world's most handsome leading man to light it for her. Cary let her hold it for some time. Finally he said in a perfect Cary Grant tone, "My dear, you are a very beautiful, young lady. Smoking is not beautiful. You may smoke if you wish, but you will have to light it yourself."

She lit it, took one puff, put it out … and probably never smoked again. Cary said we made a nice couple and that he would like to send us out on the town, dinner at Maxwell Plum and any shows we wanted to see. Then he suggested that the two of us get married and have some beautiful children. The beautiful lady remembered she had to catch a late train to Philadelphia so the date would have to be another time. That night, I was Cary's guest at Maxwell Plum, but my date was my old pal and *Genii* Magazine artist, Mickey O'Malley. Cary's New York address was the penthouse of the Warwick Hotel. There was another apartment on the top floor that was available only to Cary's guests.

Cary had to leave for London the next day but he let me use the apartment for as long as I wanted to stay in New York. Since the whole trip was planned over a couple of martinis the day before, I really hadn't given much thought about how long I was going to be there or how I was going to get back to Los Angeles. It was an unforgettable experience.

Another night, in 1971, I asked Cary if he would like to run over to the Ivar Theater in Hollywood where Bob Lauher, the Sherman Brothers, and I were doing a musical called *Victory Canteen*. It was about intermission time and I knew the cast would get a morale boost by his visit. They were still getting over the effects of the Sylmar earthquake. Cary and I jumped in my pickup truck, which happened to be parked outside the Castle, and went over to the theater. Cary graciously said "hello" to each and every member of the astonished cast and then announced to the crowd: "Milt and I have to be going now ... we have to take the truck back to the Castle."

Al Flosso & Cary Grant

Some of our senior magicians will remember a wonderful character by the name of Al Flosso. Al performed on our 14th Annual *It's Magic!* in 1968. He was one of the best kids' entertainers I have ever seen. He was a short man in a rumpled suit who treated the kids about as pleasantly as an untipped New York waiter ... he was charming! Al ran a great magic shop on 34th Street. It was one of New York's oldest stores originally called "Martinka's." Many years ago, shortly after the Castle opened in 1963, I was staying at the venerable old New Yorker's Hotel on 34th Street and realized I was across the street from Flosso's. I decided to pay a surprise visit to this living legend in magic. He didn't recognize me as I came in because he was busy shooing a kid out of the store. "You wanna buy something, sonny, I'll sell it to you. You wanna free show, get outta here!" I introduced myself and he made me feel like

a visiting potentate. He wanted to know about all his old friends that had defected to Hollywood. All of a sudden he said, "Wait here, m'boy ... there's something I want you to take back with you."

It's lucky New York doesn't have our California earthquakes. If it did, Flosso probably wouldn't have had as long a life. The back room of his shop was stacked to the ceiling with boxes of props and God knows what. One small tremor and Al would have been buried beneath a ton of magician's wax and thumb tips. He climbed up a ladder and pulled out a dust-laden box. He fished around in the box and came up with an envelope that had been marked "give to Larsen." I guess he somehow knew that sooner or later I'd pop in.

The envelope contained a wonderful card from Texas Guinan's night-club welcoming the cast of *Padlocks of 1927*. He gleefully pointed to one of the names of the cast: *Archibald Leech*. "Do you know who that is, m'boy?" "Cary Grant!" I said with the confidence of a Jeopardy winner. Al knew Cary was an active member of the Board of Directors at the Castle. He asked me to take the card back to the coast and give it to Cary.

I showed it to Cary when I returned and he got a big kick out of it. He said I could keep the card for my collection but he wrote Al a lovely letter saying how much he appreciated the gift.

George Burns

Several years ago, I was quaffing an adult beverage with John Shrum at the mezzanine bar. As usual, we were drawing plans for new ideas and changes on cocktail napkins when I got a rather strange call from the lobby. It seems some guy had wandered in off the street and was actually in the wrong club. He didn't have a guest card or anything ... but he did have a coat and tie! The host thought I might want to let him in anyway. Just as I was about to send out for a new host, he said the lost man was George Burns.

I ran down to meet this giant of show business and invited him to join us at the bar. It seems he had an appointment to meet a couple of friends at the Masquers Club around the corner. He hadn't been to the Masquers for a while and told his driver to turn into the first driveway he saw that had a sign outside proclaiming *Private Club*.

After sipping a martini and getting a quick verbal tour of the Castle, George asked if it would be all right to call his friends at the Masquers and invite them over to the Castle for dinner. While we awaited Mr. Burn's guests, I mentioned that we had quite a large collection of the early Paramount shorts that Burns and Allen had made in the 30's. He had some hilarious anecdotes about them. George also apparently worked with practically every vaudeville magician in the world ... and remembered every one of them. Brother Bill joined the party and introduced Burns to the Professor, Dai Vernon, who was just a couple of years older than George.

His guests arrived and we introduced them to our house ghost, Invisible Irma, who played several obscure songs that George liked to sing. "The Red Rose Rag" has always been one of Irma's favorites. George and his guests had a great time. Over the years, we have given out very few honorary memberships. Most of our celebrity members have joined just like you and I. Well, not like you and I ... like you. In this case, we made George Burns an honorary member on the spot. George came in often and our receptionists never asked for his ID—but we did make sure his girlfriends were over twenty-one!

Ed Wynn

My old boss, Ralph Edwards, knew I loved to talk to some of the great personalities of show business. Although I was working on *Truth or Consequences*, he was doing *This is Your Life* down the hall. Sometimes someone would have to keep the *Life* subject occupied while the stage was being set for a surprise. Ralph would love to call and ask if I'd mind taking someone to lunch or meet someone somewhere to keep him or her busy. Through Ralph Edwards, this young kid got to meet Stan

Laurel, Buster Keaton, Mack Sennett and many others. One of the most memorable afternoons of my life was a lunch I had with one of my idols. Imagine sitting across the table at the Vine Street Brown Derby with the legendary Ed Wynn? Wynn loved magic and magicians. Apparently, he was a pretty good magician himself.

There is one of his stories that I'll never forget about Mary Markham, the talent coordinator for many of Ralph's shows. Mary asked Ed a provocative question: "Do you think a comedian is born funny, or that anyone can learn to be a comedian." Mr. Wynn thought a moment and then, typically, started his answer in a roundabout way.

"First, you go out and buy two identical clay pots," he said with his proper Ed Wynn lisp. "Then you go out in the yard and fill them with exactly the same amount of dirt. Then, put them in a spot where you make sure they each get exactly the same amount of sunshine. Every day, you take a watering can and water them with exactly the same amount. One day, you will find that one of the pots has produced a beautiful flowering plant. The other one is simply a weed." Then Ed Wynn sat back, obviously pleased with his answer. Mary and I looked at one another for a moment, then Mary asked: "Mr. Wynn, what was the difference between the two pots?" "The answer is very simple," Ed lisped. "You see, only one of the pots had a seed in it!"

Several years later, after Wynn's death, I ended up with a huge collection of his memorabilia. One day I picked up the telephone to answer a call from a fellow who said he had gotten my name from Jack Blum at the Cherokee Book Shop in Hollywood. Jack had told him that I collected comedy and vaudeville material and might be interested in a collection he had for sale. He went on to say that he had a *bunch of stuff* on Ed Wynn.

When I asked what he meant by *stuff* he said he had a lot of 8x10 photos, some old radio shows, awards and mementos … that sort of thing. It really didn't sound too fascinating. I asked what he wanted for it and he said $500. I already had quite a bit of material on Wynn. Jack lived a distance away in the far reaches of that primitive area known as the San Fernando Valley. The Magic Castle® was having growing pains and my TV writing salary vanished like magic every week. I said I'd love to have it but five hundred bucks was too much for me to handle. Any chance of his lowering his price? He said he had no intention of taking a penny less but he also was in no hurry to sell the collection. If I wanted it sometime in the future, it would probably still be available.

About a year later, I found his number among the confetti on my desk. I called and asked if he still had the stuff on Ed Wynn. He did and the price, he assured me, was still $500! I figured I'd at least run out and take a look. I arrived at a nice ranch-style house, met the owner who handed me a cup of coffee. I noticed a stack of photos and a couple of nice Wynn items on his breakfast table. He said, "Take your time. I'll be watching the ball game."

"Is this it?" I asked, looking at the things on the table. He laughed and walked over to a closet door, opening it. I suddenly knew how it must have felt to be at the opening of King Tut's tomb. It was a very large closet, literally stacked to the ceiling with hundreds of photos, radio transcriptions, plaques and awards, 16mm kinescope films, posters, framed citations and letters. There were three hand-tinted framed posters on top. I'm sure I would have been happy to pay $500 for just one of them, if I had discovered it in a collector's shop. I looked at a couple of items, then returned to my host.

"No interest?" he asked. I said I just wanted to ask if his two football player-type sons would mind putting all that *stuff* in my pickup truck while we finished our coffee and I wrote out a check. And, I noted I was certainly not going to haggle on the price!

While the truck was being loaded with my new treasures, I asked him how he came to acquire the collection. He said he was a professional junk man. One day, he had noticed a bunch of trash barrels waiting for the city trash truck. He recognized the fact that these were all items relating to one man, Ed Wynn. A lady brought out another box and put it on the heap. Was she throwing all this away? She said she was tired of it cluttering up the house. He was welcome to it.

When we opened the Ed Wynn room at the Variety Arts Center downtown, Ed Wynn's actor son, Keenan Wynn became very interested in our perpetuating the name of his father. Over the years, Keenan uncovered a couple of Bekins Storage vaults containing more memorabilia and the famed *piano-bike* which was one of Wynn's favorite comedy props. Since Ed Wynn was well known as the "Texaco Fire Chief" we were able to get a couple of very generous grants from the Texaco Foundation to help maintain this collection and support the activities of the SPVA. The collection is now part of the archives of the Society for the Preservation of Variety Arts that is temporarily housed at the Castle.

Stan Laurel

Ralph Edwards knew I was a film collector and projection nut. Our little theater in the back of the family house, Brookledge, was outfitted like a professional movie house. Dual 16mm and 35mm projectors, motorized curtains, elaborate lighting ... the works! One day he called and asked if I would mind going to Stan Laurel's apartment in Santa Monica to show him how to run his film projector. Subjects on Ralph's *This Is Your Life* shows were always presented with a 16mm film of the program and a Bell & Howell 16mm sound projector on which to run it.

Would I mind meeting Stan Laurel? As one of Laurel and Hardy's greatest fans this was like asking a Catholic: "Would you mind meeting the Pope?!" I arrived at his apartment and stammered that I was the guy sent by Ralph Edwards to fix his projector. He very politely introduced me to his wife and a couple of guests. He sounded exactly like Stanley Laurel when he said he really didn't know if it was broken, he just had never tried to run it. The projector was brand new and had never been run. All I had to do was thread up the film and turn it on.

To MILT LARSEN
BEST WISHES
Stan Laurel.

It was not too much of a challenge and I found myself thinking of some way I could slow my work so I could remain in the presence of the master for a longer time. I didn't have to worry. In asking a few questions Stan found out I was a fan, an aspiring comedy writer and a magician fascinated with the British Music Hall. He invited me to join his friends as they played cards and spent the evening talking about comedy, magic and music halls. We never did get around to running his film. I doubt that he ever did. The next time I visited him several months later the projector was still set up on the table exactly where I had left it and was still threaded up and ready to start.

I had Stan sign an old photograph that I still cherish. Later, long after Stan's passing, I got to know Stan's daughter, Lois Laurel, and her charming husband, the late Tony Hawes. We had a wonderful collection of Laurel and Hardy memorabilia on display at the Variety Arts Center until its closing in 1989. Tony let me keep Stan's very own private *zipper banana,* which is in a place of honor next to Stan's signed photo in my office.

Jack Oakie

Jack Oakie was a very active member of the Magic Castle® and a great supporter of the Variety Arts. The world premiere of Mrs. Jack Oakie's musical *The Kid from Muskogee* was produced at the Variety Arts Roof Garden. Our comedy archives are dedicated to his memory. Here at the Castle it was always fun when Jack and his wife, actress Victoria Horne (who you'll remember as the dingbat daughter in Brother Bill's absolute favorite film, *Harvey*) would join Irma for a song or two. He would usually come in after the Dodgers game with baseball hat and turtleneck sweater. To him that was proper dress for the evening. Since he always looked great and happened to be a show business legend, we never asked him to put on a necktie!

Jack loved magic and his large estate in the San Fernando Valley was very close to the Dante Ranch. Both had the good sense to buy acreage in the wide-open spaces. Jack was the master of the *double take* in films; the double, triple and quadruple takes, if you will. It was fun watching him react to our Castle magicians because of his *takes* reacting to every move.

Mrs. Oakie was Jack's biggest fan. She is constantly supporting events to perpetuate his memory. She presented her *one lady show* about Jack at our Albert Peller Theater. It was a delightful evening for an invited audience as if they were guests in the Oakie home "Oakridge." Victoria was wonderful playing the part she knew so well–Mrs. Jack Oakie. The audience loved her stories and the remarkable film clips from dozens of his best pictures.

After the show she only had one complaint. There were no restrooms on the Inner Circle level. That meant she had to go up a flight of stairs and sprint a hundred foot dash to get to the ladies room on the main theater level. "Why are there no restrooms on the Peller Theater level?" she asked. I explained the ballroom, theater and library area had once been part of a parking structure that was not designed for theaters, much less restrooms. Putting in the necessary plumbing and sewage connections would cost a lot of money … Money that was nowhere to be found in the budget in the foreseeable future.

Victoria asked me to get a bid on the job and she might donate the funds for the project, under one condition: The new restroom would have to be called "The Jack Oakie Memorial Ladies Room." She explained that any time they were at the club, Jack would have her go to retrieve the car while Jack would excuse himself to go to the "ladies room." She thought it would be fitting to call the new ladies room facilities in his honor. It's certainly a tribute to the sense of humor of both of the Oakies. Mrs. Oakie's generous donation also meant the performers could finally have a backstage restroom in the Palace of Mystery Theater.

Mae West

I found a bonanza of vintage birds' eye maple when they tore down one of the buildings at Hollywood High School in the early seventies. All that

flooring became the stage at the Mayfair Music Hall, the stage of Palace of Mystery, the stage at the Variety Arts ballroom and the bar top of the Palace of Mystery Bar. I even made a bar top for Cary Grant's Beverly Hills home out of it. Believe it or not, we still had enough to make the new bar top for the *Hello Dolly/W.C. Fields' Bar*.

While I was cutting the two hundred pieces of flooring that join together as a bar upon which to place my future very dry martini, our tireless volunteer Don Nelson and I were listening to a CD of vintage Mae West songs. Don had noticed an autographed photo and a picture of Mae West and myself taken at the Mayfair Music Hall. Mae West was a member of the Magic Castle® and used to come in quite often. We would get the same call from her male secretary, "Miss West would like to attend the show tonight. As you know, she doesn't want any special attention. She would, however, like those seats at the very back of the house." How very modest and retiring for a legendary star.

When Mae arrived at the theatre, she made every effort to be *unnoticed*. Of course, she arrived in a vintage limo driven by a body builder chauffeur. She was dressed in flowing gowns. She walked to her seats as if she was descending the grand staircase at the Paris Opera House. Somehow people noticed her. At that time she was in her eighties and she still looked great. She died in 1980 at the age of 87.

Edgar Bergen

One of the nicest members who ever graced our club was Edgar Bergen. He joined the minute he heard about the Magic Castle® and came in quite often. Edgar was a devoted magician and always considered ventriloquism as the *art of illusion*. In fact, according to Candice Bergen's 1984 biography of her father, *Knock Wood*, his original billing in vaudeville was "Edgar Bergen–Voice Illusionist."

He certainly created wonderful magic every Sunday night on the CBS Radio Network when he would cause three characters to materialize. Charlie McCarthy, Mortimer Snerd and Effie Klinker were as real to people of my generation as Fibber McGee and Molly or Amos 'n Andy. Edgar was one of the founding members of an elite group of magicians in Los Angeles called *Los Magicos*. Los Magicos was an organization prominent in the late thirties and forties. Others in that club included celebrities like Chester Morris (known for his *Boston Blackie* roles on radio and films), Harold Lloyd, songwriter Bert Kalmar, and banker Bernard Giannini. There were also major forces in magic like Caryl Fleming, John Brown Cook and our father, William Larsen, Sr. Edgar Bergen died on stage in Las Vegas in 1978 at the age of seventy-five.

Harold Lloyd

The great silent film comedian, Harold Lloyd, was a great magic fan and was very active in the local magic scene, often hosting Los Magicos meetings at his huge mansion in Beverly Hills. Harold was an early member of the Castle and would drop in from time to time to share secrets with Jay Ose and the Castle regulars. One night he appeared at the Castle with his teenage daughter. We reminded him of the "No one under twenty-one" rule. He asked if an exception could be made. Bill very politely said we really couldn't break the rules, after all it was a California liquor license thing ... if we broke the rule for Harold Lloyd, how would we explain it to other members? Harold was very understanding. He and his daughter left and, unfortunately never came in again.

When Harold Lloyd died, he left his Beverly Hills mansion to the City of Beverly Hills with the idea that it would become a museum or a place where the public could enjoy the splendor of his home, which resembled a Mediterranean palace. I often wondered if he might have left his *castle* to the magicians if we hadn't turned his daughter away that fateful night.

Ralph Edwards

Not too long after we opened the Castle, my *Truth or Consequences* boss, Ralph Edwards, came in to show the club to some friends. Without my writing job and Ralph's understanding of my wanting to "moonlight" from my full-time job, there might not have been a Castle. That night Ralph also brought his teenage daughter with him. It was not an easy thing to tell my employer and the man who was almost like a second father to me, that he couldn't bring his daughter in because of the age rule. Ralph agreed that the rules were the rules and his wife, Barbara, and daughter spent an hour or so waiting in the car while Ralph gave a quick tour of the Castle to his guests.

If I had been Ralph, I might have fired myself.

Carl Ballantine

If I had a role model in show business it had to be Walt Disney but my role model in comedy magic was Carl Ballantine. When I first saw The Amazing Mr. Ballantine getting huge laughs bluffing his way through his magic, I knew comedy magic was my thing. Carl is a charter member of the Magic Castle® and is a frequent visitor. He started as a straight magician in 1938 and says he was the very first magician in Las Vegas to perform a bird act. Later he traded the birds for a feather duster and created the Amazing Mr. Ballantine character. Although he traded in his green tails many years ago to become one of Hollywood's most active character comedians; he'll still bring out the old act for very special occasions. He is one of the world's funniest magicians.

Mayor Sam Yorty

Sam Yorty was the Mayor of Los Angeles for three terms. It has always been our custom to make the Mayor an honorary member of the club. We usually assume it's a nice political gesture. In Sam's case, he loved the Castle and would often bring guests to the club. He continued as a very active member until his passing in 1999. He was a Friday lunch regular and he was always "Mayor Sam" to our employees and members. The month after he lost the election to Tom Bradley we sent his newsletter to the address where he had always received it: Honorable Mayor Sam Yorty, City Hall, City of Los Angeles, California. We received the envelope back a few days later. Stamped on the envelope was "Unknown at this address." How soon they forget.

General Schwarzkopf

Shortly after the Gulf War we had the very delightful experience of showing the wonders of the Magic Castle® to General H. Norman Schwarzkopf. The Academy of Magical Arts made the General Honorary Magician of the Century for his magic in making the war in Iraq disappear. He is quick to credit his 541,000 apprentices who assisted him in his magic act. He is an amateur magician and is turning over his trunk of magic props to his teenage son. The General impressed us all with his knowledge of magic. He also impressed Irene Larsen with his fluent command of the German language. The general reaction of our members and guests who are used to seeing celebrities at the Castle was "what a genuine and nice man."

David Horsley

David Horsley was a little known but major figure in the early days of Hollywood and the motion picture industry. He was one of the founders of Universal Pictures. He was involved in the purchase of that almost worthless ranch land past the stagecoach stop on Cahuenga Pass.

In today's world of the National Inquirer and instant television communication our favorite Hollywood stars are exposed (one way or the other) on an almost daily basis. Back in the roaring twenties, the stars were shielded by great press agents who were handsomely paid to keep their clients names out of the papers! When a scandal did break loose it was a real doozie. Roscoe "Fatty" Arbuckle – William Desmond Taylor – Thelma Todd. Big Scandals equals Big Headlines.

David Horsley hit the lecture circuit with an illustrated lecture: "Can Anything Good Come Out of Hollywood?" Most of the back-lit hand-tinted glass slides opposite the windows in the Terrace Dining Room came from the David Horsley Collection which was donated to us by member Bill Smith. Amidst a slide of the signboard announcing the future construction of Grauman's Chinese Theatre, there are interesting photos of character real estate offices offering choice lots in Hollywood. The slides are an interesting view of Hollywood in the twenties: portraits of actresses and actors, stars homes (including Pauline Fredericks' large home on Franklin Avenue. Pauline was our "house ghost" at the Variety Arts Center.) Maybe we can get the ghost of David Horsley to drop into the Houdini Séance some evening to give us an encore of his lecture.

Ironic but True–
Martinka and the Castle

Film pioneer Jesse Lasky and Rollin B. Lane were good friends. Lane was the banker from Redlands who built the original home, which is now called the Magic Castle®. Lasky built a large home just around the corner at the top of La Brea. Lane was instrumental in arranging the financing for many of the early Lasky/DeMille epics. Lasky's success helped Lane build his grand home that would someday be home base for the world's magicians.

Jesse Lasky and Cecil B. DeMille came west on the railroad to film *The Squaw Man*. They were going to set up shop in the desert of Arizona. When the train got to Arizona, it was raining. Mr. Lasky decided to continue on until they found a desert without rain. Lasky ended up at what is now the corner of Selma Avenue and Vine Streets. Thank goodness for that train depot five miles west of Los Angeles! Other film pioneers followed Lasky to his land of sunshine in the non-existent woods where there has never been any holly. If it hadn't been for the great draught of 1905, "The Entertainment Capitol of the World" might have been in Needles, California.

Now for a bit of ironic magical history: Gus Hartz ranked as a rival of Hermann, The Great and Robert Heller during the 1880's and 1890's. With his brother, "The Great Hartz" they opened the first magic shop in New York City which later became the legendary "Martinka's." Gus had seen Robert Houdin whose performance inspired the brothers to become magicians. Gus Hartz' daughter, Fanny Hartz, married Arthur Friend. He was a Milwaukee lawyer with theatrical aspirations and he talked melodrama producers Cecil B. DeMille and Jesse Lasky into forming the Lasky Famous Players Company that pioneered the making of movies in Hollywood. It very well may have been a magician who made the first move in a chain of events that led to the creation of The Magic Castle®.

Growing Pains

The Need For More Space

The day Tom Glover handed me the key to the front door of the old house, I remember standing in the front main room, thinking how the entire house seemed huge. It was immense. Would we ever need all this room? Would there ever be a day when we could actually have a need for the entire second floor? It didn't take too long to determine that we constantly needed more and more space.

Soon, we were trying to find more usable areas in the original old mansion. I started looking at former broom closets. The kitchen had been designed for a family residence and was much too small for the number of dinners we were serving nightly. We started tacking on little additions here and there, but we were running out of space.

Haunted Wine Cellar

Under a portion of the house was a typical, full basement where the original, old furnaces and storerooms were located. About two-thirds of the area, however was crawl space with only about five feet of headroom. Every old haunted house should have a dank and cobwebbed wine cellar, so we decided to build one. Half barrels made great cocktail tables and one end of the room became a stage, simply because we couldn't move the building foundation.

Our new *Haunted Wine Cellar* opened in June of 1965. The night before we opened the cellar, the NBC moonlight special effects crew came in at closing time and worked all morning, filling the room with realistic-looking studio cobwebs. The next day, we went in to admire their work. The janitors had done a great job of removing every one of those pesky cobwebs! The haunted wine cellar was a fun room. It was a great place for impromptu magic but magicians were hesitant about performing on its little, cramped stage.

Before Berry Lee became a standard comedy magic act in Las Vegas, and before he owned his first Rolls Royce and yacht, he worked for about a year as a parking lot attendant at the Castle. Berry was quick to notice that the magicians were considerably warmer than the parking lot guys on cold nights were. He bought some magic props and offered to do his new act in the Haunted Wine Cellar. Cary Grant loved Berry's act and brought his friends down to the cellar to see him. Cary's friends were the likes of Kirk Kerkorian and Major Riddle, the owner of the Dunes Hotel in Las Vegas. With Cary's blessing and encouragement, Berry's career slipped into high gear. When the other magicians noticed Berry getting stellar audiences in the wine cellar, they also wanted to work the room. After a few years, we turned the little wine cellar into our first Palace of Mystery theatre.

Mama Cat

Obviously the little stage in the basement was not large enough for big stage illusions. We might see an occasionally Zigzag or a guillotine illusion but that was about it on the extravaganza scale. One magician who brought his own style of spectacle to that stage was Shimada. Shimada came to United States from Japan and played the *It's Magic!* show a record number of times. He did his beautiful parasol act with birds and lighted torches at the Magic Castle®. Spectators would sometimes get a little nervous as the flames seemed to be licking the black cloth ceiling on the little stage.

One night that ceiling seemed to be lower than usual. On further examination we found that a neighborhood cat had decided that the ceiling would make a nice hammock for her to magically produce a litter of kittens. Shimada's torch performances were suspended until the kittens could be moved!

Closing the Cellar

The closing of the cellar was a night to remember. In those days, we used to close the Castle every year for two weeks in September. The night we closed the wine cellar was on the eve of a two-week's closing. We had decided to make the cellar into a real little theatre. John Shrum and I knew what we were going to do, but nobody else realized we were going to totally gut the room and start over.

My years of writing practical jokes for *Truth or Consequences* created a certain amount of brain damage. I couldn't let the opportunity for a typical *Truth or Consequences* "Strikes Again" joke to slip past. I announced that I would like to be the last act to play the old room. Members had seen my "magic carpenter act." They knew I chopped up cards and ropes and broke glass. They also knew I would stoop to new lows of destruction for a few cheap laughs.

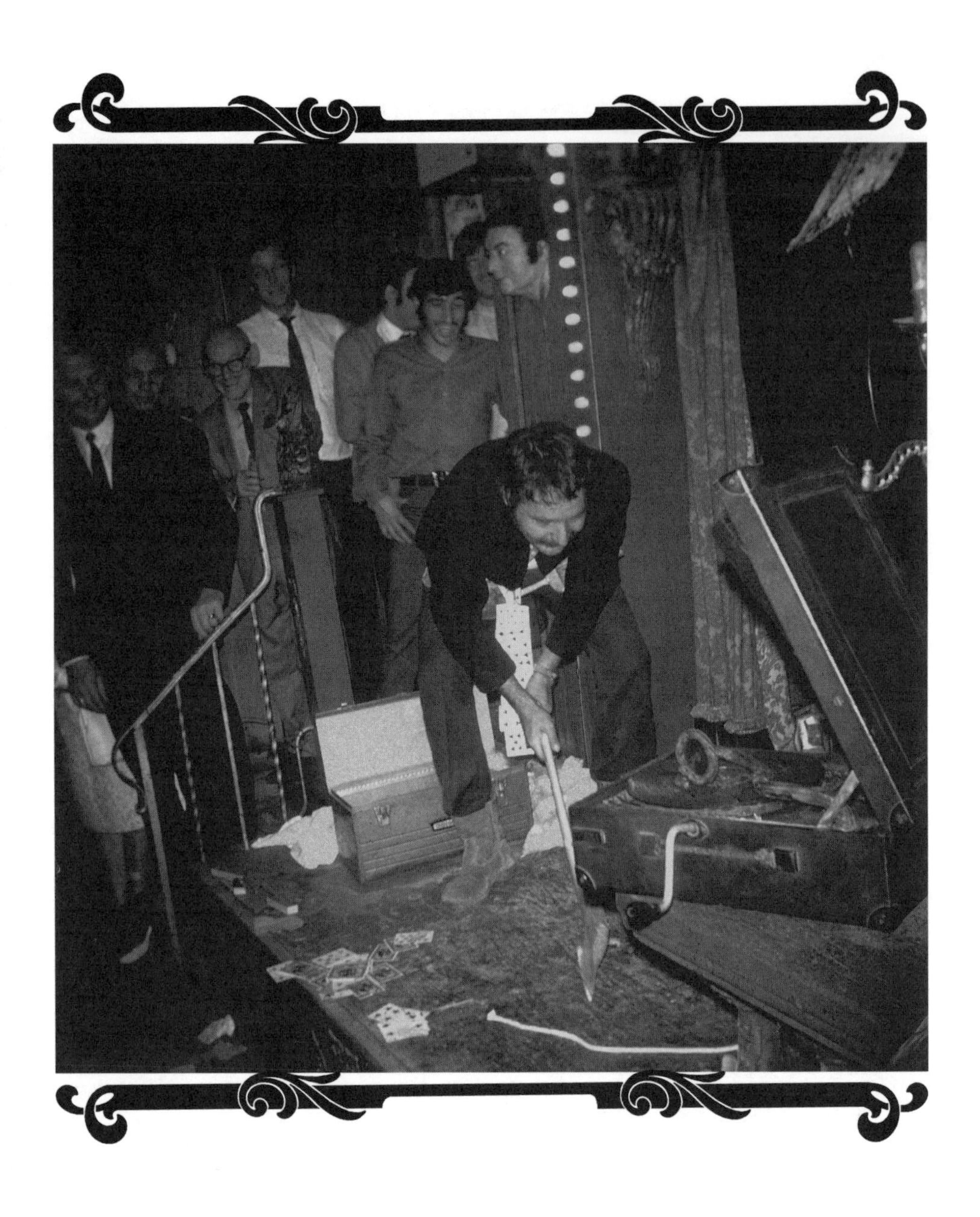

That night the room was packed with members and unsuspecting guests. The act started in its usual way, but then it started getting slightly out of hand. Instead of a little hatchet, I used a regulation fire ax. In raising it over my head, I "accidentally" tore out part of the sheet rock ceiling. I did a "cut and restored board" and Skil-sawed right through the floors.

As the debris started falling, some of the audience edged towards the exit. What was Milt thinking? We nearly lost Dick Colyar, our bartender, who had sneaked backstage to watch the act. I didn't know he was there and let the ax fly through the wall within inches of him. As far as I know, he never tried to sneak in the back way again! (Maybe our hosts could use that trick.) Two weeks later the new Palace of Mystery opened. Today it's hard to believe that was our biggest showroom for several years. It had forty-nine seats and a tiny stage.

Owl Bar

Crescent City is about as far as you can go north in the State of California. It's at the very top of the state and the last seaport before you get to Oregon. What does this geography lesson have to do with the Magic Castle®? Well, Crescent City was once the home of a rough-and-ready waterfront wrestling arena. It was wiped out in a disastrous tidal wave in the late fifties. Among the victims of the flooding waters was a grand old mahogany bar that had been shipped *'round the horn* in the 1890's to provide a resting place for the elbows of many a drunken sailor.

Ernie Evans, our beloved junk man, asked if we needed a slightly waterlogged bar. The base had rotted away and the veneer was peeling, but the price was right. This was about a year after we opened the Castle and we really didn't need a big antique bar. The bar I had built in the main lounge seemed to satisfy all our needs. But then, how could we turn down a genuine Brunswick, Balke, and Collender Patented bar?

At that time, Bobby Lauher and I were writing *The Mickey Finn Show* for NBC. They wanted to re-create Fred Finn's saloon in San Diego so I rented them the old bar. The studio painstakingly restored the bar and it became part of the set for the run of the show. Then I used it as a practical bar in the lobby of the Music Box Theatre for *They Called It Vaudeville*. When that show closed, our dear friend Spencer Quinn needed a bar for a beer/banjo bar he was opening on Sunset Boulevard. We loaned the bar to Spencer for a couple of years. He sold the business and we ended up with the bar again.

Guess what? Dean Martin needed a bar for his show so back to NBC it went. They added the dozens of little peanut light bulbs.

The *Heavy-handed Harry Bar* was then situated between the Houdini Room and the Cherub Room. In the old house that bar used to be a bathroom. We found out early in life at the Castle that bathrooms made great bars ... something about the plumbing! Heavy-handed Harry was the late Harry Wolf, a charming bartender from the old school. Harry kept the club *non-profit* for years.

Back in the early days of the Castle, we used to close for two weeks after Labor Day. During those two weeks we would usually make some dramatic change that necessitated closing down the whole joint. On one two-week reconstruction period, we installed the Brunswick, Balke, and Collender bar on the mezzanine. Two weeks later, we were done. It looked like it had always been there. One of the things that amused us was the innocent statement made by many a customer: "Aren't you lucky to have found an old house with a bar like this on the mezzanine."

Incidentally, few people notice that there is one single step in the service hallway behind the mezzanine bar. If you walk clockwise from the dining room through the service area you will step down one step into the hallway. If you continue down the hall and back through the dining room, there is never a step up. By like token, walk counter-clockwise through the same area and you will have to take one step up, but there is never another step down! We have never been able to explain this.

All the floors are level and yet there is this one step. Theoretically, if you walk around the circle fifteen times, you will be upstairs. There is also a complete finished floor one foot below the floor of that hallway, apparently another small miscalculation by the carpenters at the time. Coincidentally, at the time the corridor was built, we noticed several shortages in the wine inventory in the mezzanine bar.

Walt Disney

If I had a role model it would have to be Walt Disney. Maybe that's why I grew the mustache. I had the pleasure of being at Disneyland on its opening night. Back then, everyone called it "Walt's Folly." Pacific Ocean Park had just gone belly-up and, after all, who would build a huge amusement park out in the God-forsaken wilderness of Anaheim?

One night I was visiting Disneyland with Barbara Logan and we somehow ended up at the back of the park when they announced it was closing time. We ambled towards the main gate as they started turning out the lights. While we were walking down Main Street USA I noticed a man strolling alone, pausing now and then to look into the windows. I recognized him as my idol, Walt Disney.

We kept our distance because I wanted to see where he was going. As we neared the front gate, he said hello to a couple of guards and walked over to a waiting live steam engine. He got in the cab, put on the engineer's hat and drove off, just one man alone in his own personal train. As we left the park, that train was the only moving thing in Disneyland. It struck me that this man had built the world's greatest park for kids, but the biggest kid of all was Walt Disney!

Years later I was at the Disney Studios visiting my old pals, Bob and Dick Sherman. Their office was on the same floor as "Uncle Walt's." As we got on the elevator, Walt and a short man in a black suit joined us. We exchanged pleasantries and Walt asked how everything was going at the Castle. After they walked off, Dick Sherman commented: "That was the guy who built Disneyland. No, not Walt ... the other guy!" Then he went on to explain that every bank in the world had turned Walt down for his insane pipe dream. The man in the black suit was the one banker who convinced his bank, the Bank of America, to go along with the Walt's idea.

Walt & Roy, Bill & Milt

The success of the Magic Castle® made the front page of the Wall Street Journal with an article that compared Bill and I to Walt Disney and his brother Roy. I was delighted at the comparison. The article really irritated our landlord Tom Glover, since it kept referring to Bill and I as owners of the property. Tom was very proud of his role in the success of the Castle and hated it when the press passed over him in articles.

In every interview, Bill and I would point out that the Glover family owned the Castle property and we were operating under a lease in close association with Tom Glover. Invariably, the final version would come out, "The Magic Castle® owners, Bill and Milt Larsen." Like Walt and Roy, my brother and I made a great team. I knew how to work the typewriter and hammer; Bill knew how to operate the adding machine and cash register. The Disney Brothers had their Magic Kingdom and the Brothers Larsen had their Magic Castle®.

Bill Larsen-The Prez

Bill graduated from Occidental College and went to USC Law School. I went directly from high school to gag writing. Bill was a straight "A" student and I was an "A" student in things like woodshop, electric shop, stage, play production and drama. I was a lousy student in everything else. I flunked English twice on my way to becoming a successful writer. Bill was three years older, which meant my high school teachers expected my brother's high performance from his always-joking, shy-away-from-boring-subjects brother.

Bill had been the stage manager at Los Angeles High School and that was one area where I could ride on his laurels. I was the L.A. High stage manager for all three years of high school. I loved the stage and all those years of playing old vaudeville houses paid off. Where Bill had been an excellent stage *manager*, I was an excellent *stage* manager. I loved building sets and working the machinery of the stage. I would get to school early in the morning and usually leave when it got dark. My management-oriented brother would coordinate the efforts of his student crew. I would hammer, saw, glue, paint and get the job done. Let's face it, Bill was the better stage manager. He was a born manager.

Bill had managed the Thayer Magic store on La Brea Avenue for Dad and then went to CBS-TV working his way up through the "cost control" department to become one of the network's top Associate Producers. During Bill's seventeen years at CBS-TV, he handled the production finances for their top shows including *Playhouse 90*, *Climax* and *The Danny Kaye Show*. In January of 1968, Bill made a very difficult choice. He was doing three full-time jobs as well as trying to raise an ever-growing family. He was the editor of *Genii* Magazine, an executive at CBS with an ever-increasing schedule and the President of the Academy of Magical Arts.

In the January 1968 *Genii* editorial, Bill mentions the fact that his CBS job had become very time consuming and, even though it paid well, the pay against the time consumed "wasn't all that good!" He goes on to say another factor was " ... the formation and tremendous growth of the Magic Castle®. Started with spit and Milt's hammer, it now grosses over a half-million dollars a year. Gross, I say, because neither Milt nor I am making a living from the Magic Castle® ... but we would like to think we can when all the back bills and rents are paid."

He announced that, when his contract ended, he would resign from CBS to devote full time to *Genii*, the Magic Castle®, The Academy of Magical Arts, and our other magic projects. It was a very difficult decision for Bill at the time because he was clearly in position to become a top executive with the network. But his great interest in life, like his father's before him, was the love of magic. And he never regretted that decision.

Rubbing the Lamp

When Bill Larsen Sr. and Geri Larsen started *Genii* Magazine back in 1936 I was five years old and my brother was eight. Dad was only thirty years old when he started *Genii* and I was thirty when I met Tom Glover and started the ball rolling for the Magic Castle®. Prior to *Genii* Dad and T. Page Wright had written dozens of articles for Dr. Wilson's *Sphinx* magazine.

The publication of a major magazine of magic on the Pacific Coast was a major breakthrough in the United States where most magic was centered in New York and Chicago. *Genii* said to the world: "Hey, there is a lot of magic activity on the west coast!" After Dad died my mother carried on with *Genii* and then turned the publishing and editing reins over to brother Bill Larsen. After Bill's passing Irene and their children kept the *Genii* lamp burning. In 1998, after 62 years of continuous publication, the family sold *Genii* to Richard Kaufman of Washington D.C. who is carrying on with the magazine today.

Bill and his wife Irene promoted the Academy of Magical Arts and the Magic Castle® through the pages of *Genii* and became the club's Ambassadors of good will attending most major magic conventions throughout the world. Over the years we have received wonderful awards and honors but the highest reward the Larsen family has received is the knowledge that we have been a major factor in promoting the art of magic in the world. Because of *Genii*, the *It's Magic!* annual stage shows, The Academy of Magical Arts and the Magic Castle®, we have helped create a new and continuing respect for magic. To have young professional magicians say something that we did many years ago influenced them to follow a career in magic is worth more than all the trophies and citations in the world.

Arlene

On August 28, 1989 after a half century of bachelorhood, I married Arlene Zamiara. Who is Arlene? Is she some sort of gorgeous heiress? Did she own Rolls Royces and polo ponies? Nope. She came from a modest family who all worked in the family machine shop in Lakewood. I met Arlene when she was working as the wardrobe mistress on *Truth or Consequences*.

Arlene has a long list of credits on other TV shows including *Laugh In*. I asked her to do some of the costumes for our Mayfair Music Hall revues. She had a rare knack of making very expensive looking costumes for next to nothing. My kind of gal! She still makes her own dresses and fancy gowns when we go to parties. Why spend $1,000 when you can make the same dress for $29.95? We worked together and played together. Love had crept into my life. Our relationship grew into an *almost married* life.

We had decided to get married and we got a license in Santa Barbara. I told Arlene I didn't want a big, huge, fancy wedding and she agreed. We talked about the possibility of getting hitched in Las Vegas or on a cruise ship. When it came to the wedding I did it my way. The wedding was a total surprise to Arlene, her family, my family and to the crowd of family and close friends who thought it was simply a beach party at my home in Santa Barbara.

All those years of training as a writer with Ralph Edwards paid off. I learned one thing working on *Truth or Consequences*: "The best way to keep a secret is to keep your mouth shut!" Only two people knew we were going to get married. My mother, Geri Jaffe, and I only told her a couple of days before the occasion, and Dr. John Booth, who officiated at the ceremony. Most of our friends think of John as the prolific writer of magic books and articles. Arlene had no idea John is also very well known in the ministry world. Dr. Booth had performed a number of weddings at the Castle and I was impressed with his moving and beautiful ceremony.

My oldest and closest friend, Richard M. Sherman, was notified on the spot that he was to act as best man. Arlene's sister, Christine, was maid of honor. (I had planned to have two "best men" but Brother Bill and Irene had car trouble and arrived halfway through the wedding. It would have helped if I had told them about it.) The wedding also started late because Chris showed up Sunday morning without her mother who had decided to pass on the party. That's when I had to tell Arlene that "today is the day." Ah, the best laid plans…

It was also the first marriage for Arlene. She is a great partner in life and spends a large amount of time with the Magic Castle® volunteers turning the Castle and events at the club into really special events. Actually I got a pretty good deal when I married Arlene. I also found the perfect assistant in her sister, Christine. She handles all my day-to-day administrative work in my offices next to the Castle and the very big job of coordinating publicity for our yearly productions of *It's Magic!* Chris also does a great deal of the work on the Castle's monthly newsletter, which I volunteered to edit after the passing of Don Damaskin. That's very typical. I volunteer and Chris gets to do all the work!

Arlene's Leg

Not too long after we were married Arlene fractured her kneecap. My nephew Dante Larsen and his dog Wilma were visiting us at our home in Santa Barbara. Wilma was a cute little dog who was not allowed in china shops because of an over-active tail. We had a huge dog by the name of "Dawg." He was a mixed breed of Doberman, German Shepherd and, we suspect, horse.

Wilma and Dawg were cavorting on the lawn when, all of a sudden, Dawg decided to run where Arlene was standing. Arlene spent the next several months learning the world of very uncomfortable casts, wheelchairs, crutches and canes with a fractured kneecap. Our home has lots of stairs, making life very difficult for Arlene. She never blamed Dawg. After all, he was just playing.

Outwardly, Arlene is not a mean and vengeful person. A few months later, Dawg must have gotten his foot caught in a pocket in Arlene's station wagon. A trip to the vet proved that Dawg had broken his little toe. Arlene had to care for a big dog while in a very cumbersome cast. One day I saw Dawg sitting on the very spot where he had knocked over Arlene. The dog looked pitiful but I couldn't help noticing a slight smile on Arlene's face.

Yamashiro

When Arlene and I were in Japan, we took the bullet train to Kyoto. Our hotel was directly across from the very impressive Imperial Palace. Looking across the City of Kyoto to the hills beyond, I kept looking at one beautiful hill and remarked to Arlene that it reminded me of our hill in Hollywood. I kidded that all it needed was a Magic Castle® and a Yamashiro.

Later I was looking at a map and retracing visits to the fabulous temples shown to us by our gracious hosts Masatoshi Furota and his wife, Kazue. I decided to look for that hill. I found it on the map and it is called "Shiro Yama." Shiro is Japanese for Castle or Palace. Yama means mountain. I guess Tom and Lucy Glover must have admired that hill too!

A Pig in the Park

Over the years, we've been approached by various artists to display their works in the Castle. If it is a nice piece of art on the subject of magic, we gladly accept it as a donation. One day we were introduced to a sculptor who showed us a sketch of a piece of art he wanted to create and donate to the Magic Castle®. It would depict a Lance Burton-ish magician in a cape and would be a fifteen-foot high statue… made completely of scrap auto parts! The whole fountain area needed a new life so we agreed he could create the sculpture as long as he did the complete installation. Placing the sculpture required a crane and a new foundation.

We didn't see it until the official unveiling. The immediate reaction was one of total astonishment. Not exactly the kind of astonishment an artist would garner. The sculpture was totally contemporary which clashed horribly with the Victorian mansion. The real turn-off was that most people thought it looked more like a pig than a magician. I would like to say a few people didn't like it, but the fact is, everyone hated it!

It stayed around longer than it should have. For one thing we had promised the sculptor that it would remain in place for a certain length of time and a deal is a deal. Then he was going to take it out but never quite got around to it. When we finally removed it, we shot a video of the event and ran it at our awards banquet as if it was a live shot of the big piggy finale. Needless to say, it got a huge ovation.

Aries-a Bad Sign

I'm not really big on astrology. Sure, I read Sidney Omarr every day and a lot of the advice really does seem to hit home. I understand one of the traits of an Aries person is that they are very creative and like to start things. They are natural entrepreneurs and innovators. Once the project is off and running, the proper Aries person likes to go on to something more challenging. My Brother Bill was a Taurus. That sign is a flow through sign. That's why Bill and I made a great combination.

Bill used to love to tell the story of how he and I worked together. He said, "My Brother Milt starts building a little snowball at the bottom of a huge hill. He works and works and pushes that snowball all the way to the top of the hill. Then he pushes the snowball over the top and it rolls down the hill getting bigger and bigger, almost wiping out the villages below." Bill would chase the snowball down the hill and save the villages and the people. Then he would look up and there would be his brother at the top of the hill with another snowball!

In the late sixties, I had time on my hands, a dangerous situation. By the late sixties, we had once again run out of space. About that time, I had gone to Tom Glover with the idea of saving one of the old Spanish-style buildings to create another club/restaurant. I also wanted to start another restaurant idea on the land between his Yamashiro Hotel and the Magic Castle® where guests would dine in European compartment cars, apparently travelling through Turkey while the waiters and waitresses enacted a show I called the *Orient Express*. To show my intentions, I even bought two full-sized railroad cars at the legendary MGM auction. (That's where I also bought a 53' scale model of the Queen Minnie, but that's another story.)

Tom really liked the idea but he pointed out this was still a residential zone and the idea of turning it into some sort of Disneyland might not auger too well with the neighborhood. Of course, he was right but it still would have been a lot of fun.

We started planning a new dining terrace to expand the existing second story porch and some new kitchen service facilities. That major expansion area opened in November 1971. I was still producing the annual *It's Magic!* shows at the Wilshire Ebell Theatre as well as some other fun one-night extravaganzas. Some of our stage shows were *The Legends of Jazz* (bringing back true jazz greats in association with Floyd Levin), *Where It Was* (presenting the last of the really great ragtime artists in association with Richard Zimmerman), *The Sounds of Silents* (silent movies with a full orchestra on stage), and Bob Lauher, the Sherman Brothers and I collaborated on a new musical comedy, *Victory Canteen*.

The Hollywood Christmas Parade of 1970 found us very well represented (thanks to publicist Shirley Carroll.) We had a Venice Pier Tram featuring girls in card costumes, a dozen magicians from the Magic Castle®, and a double deck bus with a big Dixieland band on the upper deck. To top it off, we had a World War II convoy led by banjo player Spencer Quinn in a jeep driven by Professor David E. Bourne. Then came a truck full of jitterbugging dancers and another truck with Patty Andrews of the Andrews Sisters singing to our 1940's jukebox.

Hail Britannia

Dr. Tom Heric, John Shrum and I had talked about the idea of creating a turn-of-the-century British Music Hall in Hollywood. Both Tom and I were fascinated with vaudeville and variety and thought the time might be right. I was also thinking about making the unused basement area in the Castle into a British pub. Tom convinced me to go to London to look at music halls. It was my first trip to London but Tom had spent a great deal of time there, interning at a London hospital.

My mother, Geri Larsen, had gotten married to radio/TV personality Art Baker, in 1968, at the grand old Victorian Russell Hotel in London. I suggested we stay there. Dr. Tom would have none of it, he said it was an old firetrap! We agreed to stay at the London Hilton. I was awakened in the middle of the night by the sound of fire wagons and a knock on the door. An elderly bellman said, in his very best Eric Blore imitation, not to be alarmed. There was a fire in the hotel causing acrid smoke but it was quite under control. No need to panic or leave the room. I went back to watch the red lights from our 27th floor window. Tom slept through the whole event.

In the morning, I mentioned that the Russell Hotel seemed like a good idea since, firetrap or not, it was probably safer than the Hilton was. Then I told him about the fire. He didn't believe me. As we walked down Hyde Park to Marble Arch, the British newsies' billboard-sized headlines proclaimed: "Fire at Hilton." Ah, revenge is sweet.

Mayfair Music Hall

By 1973 I had simply run out of space to create anything new at the Magic Castle® and Tom Glover decided not to give me the entire hill to play with. Dr. Tom Heric and I had talked about the idea of creating a British music hall. We looked at a couple of buildings in the Hollywood area but they all had too many problems.

One day I was napping on my favorite spot at Will Rogers beach. I packed up my towel and sun tan lotion, and headed home. There was some kind of problem at the tunnel entrance to the freeway, so I drove up the California Street incline and figured I would use Santa Monica Boulevard as an alternate route. Suddenly I noticed the Mayfair Theater. For the first time I noticed the theater must have once had a stage. You can always spot a legitimate theater by the telltale stage house or fly loft shape. Of even more importance I noticed a small sign in a second floor window: "For Lease."

It seems that sign referred only to an upstairs office but the current lease with the theater operator was about to run out and he might be willing (Yeah, anxious!) to sell out early. We struck a deal and ended up with a ten-year lease and one helluva challenge.

The original theater was built in 1911 and opened as the Santa Monica Opera House. The name soon changed to the Majestic Theater. It originally had 600 seats and a full stage. The Majestic ran three acts of vaudeville and a silent movie until the advent of talkies in the late twenties. When sound came in the stage went out. They tore out the stage and moved the proscenium to the back wall with just enough space behind the screen for the big loud speakers. In the fifties the name was changed to the Mayfair Theater and it was modernized with typical cottage cheese dropped ceilings in the lobby. It was still a pretty little theater.

John Shrum, Tom Heric and I formed Old London Music Hall, Inc. Brother Bill elected to pass on the project to devote his full time to the Magic Castle® and *Genii* Magazine although he was one of our greatest fans and supporters.

When we took over the Mayfair Theater in Santa Monica it had been modernized. What charm it may have had when it was built in 1911 had been sacrificed to the Great God of Plastic and tacky curtain cover-up. The three partners, Dr. Tom Heric, John Shrum and I, sat in the back of the theater and pondered the best way to turn this swell old barn into a place where we could put on a show. As always the solution came from "Mr. Junk," our old friend Ernie Evans who ran Scavenger's Paradise and saved architectural artifacts one step ahead of the wrecking ball. Ernie called and said they were about to demolish the Belmont Theater and we might be able to use some of the stage hardware.

The Belmont was one of L.A.'s fine old movie palaces. It stood at 1st and Vermont and had been built in the early twenties. Anyone remember the Bimini Baths and the Palomar Ballroom? They were neighbors. 1st and Vermont was easily accessible by the big electric trolleys and was considered a resort on the west side of town. John and I went over to meet Ernie and his son, Rick, at the Belmont. There it was. Everything we needed! Gold leaf boxes, great staff plaster columns, paneling—a Victorian theater do-it-yourself kit. We told Ernie we didn't want the Belmont's stage hardware ... we wanted the whole Belmont interior! Soon Ernie's trucks were unloading tons of ornamental plaster and goodies to the Mayfair.

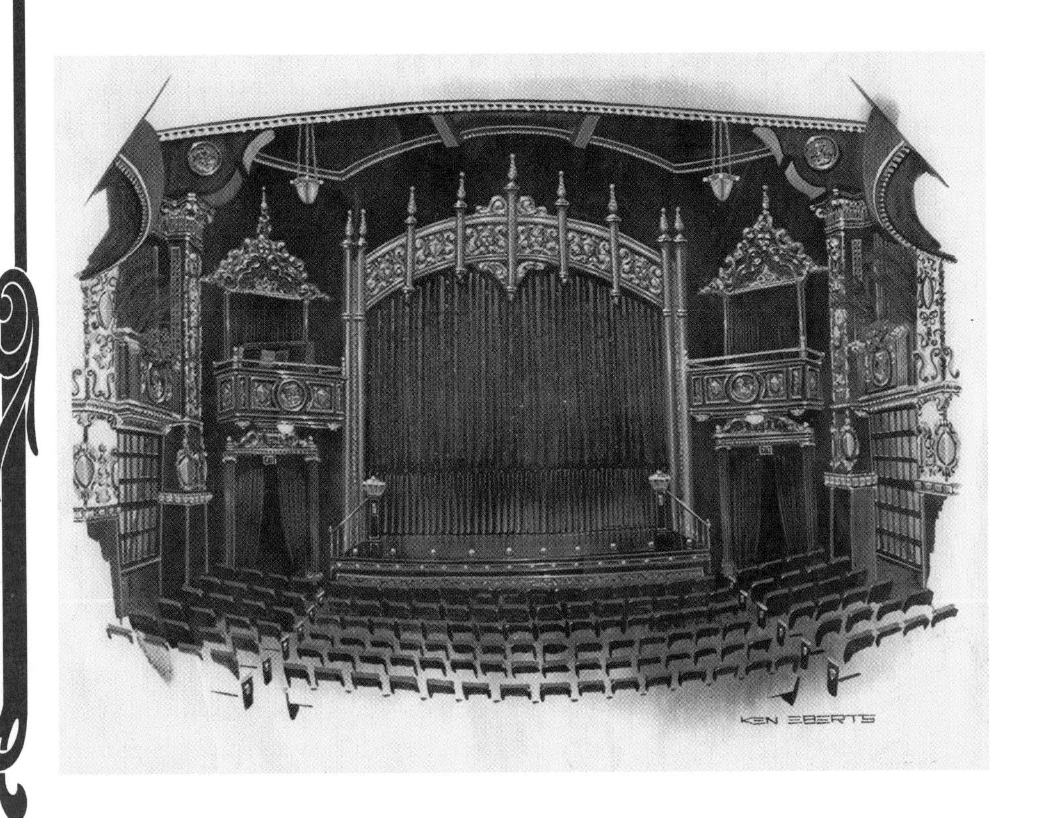

We had to get a special permit from the Santa Monica Building and Safety Department to mount these unique treasures to the walls. It was quite a trick but, when we were done, people marveled at the fact that we had "uncovered" a lost Victorian Music Hall.

The Mayfair Music Hall in Santa Monica opened on October 16, 1973. The Mayfair British music hall shows ran for seven years and twenty-one editions. The Mayfair shows were great fun. "Mr. Chairman" for most of those years was Mr. Bernard Fox who was very well known as "Dr. Bombay" on the Bewitched TV series and "Colonel Crittenden" on *Hogans Heroes*. Many magicians and vaudeville acts appeared at the Mayfair along with an incredibly talented stock company.

The owner of the Mayfair was a wonderful gentleman by the name of Carl Tegner. His father had built the theater back in 1911. Carl loved the idea of restoring the theater and was really supportive in everything we did. Unfortunately Carl passed away and his nephew took over the real estate management business. We wanted to buy the property but it was not for sale.

I got involved in the Variety Arts Center building downtown and sold my interests in the Mayfair. The theater suffered some damage in the Northridge earthquake and they used that as an excuse to gut the theater of all the Victorian elegance we had worked so hard to create. Today the Mayfair is simply an empty shell of a building but we'll always treasure the memories of those very happy seven years.

Mrs. Winchester

Brother Bill used to call me "Mrs. Winchester," referring to the lady in San Jose who never stopped building. After completing the new showroom annex I, once again, found myself with no space to expand at the Castle. The Mayfair Music Hall was doing well and I was writing the game segments for the Jim Nabors Show on TV. Bill, the Board of Directors and a great staff ran the Magic Castle®. I really needed another challenge.

I spotted a "For Sale" sign. The old Friday Morning Club was a magnificent edifice on Figueroa. I had remembered performing there as a kid with the Larsen family. It was a 60,000 square foot building and it needed saving.

In 1975 I headed a group that formed a non-profit organization called *The Society for the Preservation of Variety Arts*. Our goal was to find a home for my large collection of vaudeville material and similar collections. We started looking for a home. The building seemed perfect for our needs and the price was right. This was 1977, just before the big land boom. I always loved the line attributed to Joe Frisco: "I'm not worried about a depression … I went broke in the boom!"

The story of my involvement with the Variety Arts and its Chapter 11 Bankruptcy will have to wait for yet another book (or a pretty funny movie). It did keep me pretty well occupied for the next eleven years and, I might add, pretty well broke!

Memorable Magicians

My Favorites

If there were a magician within a few hundred miles of Southern California, Dad would haul the family off to see the act. In addition to the steady parade of famous magicians who seemed to live at our Pasadena home and then later at the Brookledge, I got to see acts like Cardini, "Think-a-drink" Hoffmann, Gala-Gali, Paco Miller, Fu Manchu, A. Robbins "The Banana Man" and a host of others.

I guess my favorite had to be Dante. He was the ultimate magician. He looked like a magician, talked like a magician, acted like a magician, and his magic was pure magic. Running a close second in the big illusion show department was Harry Blackstone Sr. Blackstone also had all the same qualities. Dante was more of a magic revue while Blackstone was like watching a whirlwind vaudeville show. They were both great in every sense of the word. Both Dante and Blackstone used to play their full evening shows at the Biltmore Theater next to the Biltmore Hotel in downtown Los Angeles. It was a fabulous theater in the tradition of all New York playhouses. It had balconies, galleries, ornate boxes and a great dome from which Dante could hang his triple trunk illusion. Blackstone also played the grand old Orpheum theater at Ninth and Broadway. This was his vaudeville stage revue and I got to see it when I was a teenager.

Josephine Baker

There was an article in the paper about two films being produced on the life of the great French singer and dancer Josephine Baker. Our old friend and SPVA/Castle member Gene Bell used to appear as the tap dancing opening act for this incredible artist. The first time I saw them was at the old RKO Hillstreet Theater in downtown Los Angeles. I had a few of her old 78's. The records were made in the late 1920's and thirties. I was a mere youth and she was an old lady. Actually she was probably pushing sixty but … when you are a mere youth!

Watching Josephine Baker perform was a lesson in showmanship. At one point she swirled around and knocked over the microphone stand with her gorgeous gown. She spent about five minutes picking it up, caressing it, kissing it—the audience cheered at her handling of this awkward accident. She felt sorry for a photographer who had to crouch in the aisle to take pictures. She stopped in the middle of a song to talk to him and left the stage, returning with an old bentwood chair that she gave to him so he could sit down and enjoy the show.

The audience cheered. She rewarded a guy in the audience who was accidentally hit by a flying piece of her costume by giving him her shoe in which she inserted a small bottle of champagne. The audience roared! She made eye contact with every member of the packed theater. We all felt we were seeing a once in a lifetime performance.

The next night, I went back to see her again. It was then that I realized the full meaning of her showmanship. Again she swirled and accidentally knocked over the mike stand. Again she felt sorry for the photographer, stopped her song and went off to get the chair. Again that piece of her costume flew off and again she gave away the champagne and her shoe ... and again and again and again the audience roared and cheered their approval. In her whole act there wasn't one wasted movement.

Moretti

In the long run of the annual *It's Magic!* shows we always tried to bring new and unusual acts to Los Angeles. Bill and I would occasionally see a foreign act that would be so good we would extend an open invitation to play *It's Magic!* any time that act could work out the logistics. One year we saw such an act on a show at the F.I.S.M. World Congress of Magic in Vienna.

The act was "Moretti." Moretti looked like a wrestler with a shaved head and no neck, but he moved with the grace of a butterfly. He did highly original magic illusions combined with a crossbow marksmanship stunt that was an absolute showstopper. We had to have Moretti on *It's Magic!* Moretti spoke almost no English so Bill's wife, Irene, explained in her best fluent German, that anytime Moretti could get to Los Angeles in October or November he would be booked. Anytime!

One day a few years later we got a letter from Moretti. The Moretti's would be available to work the *It's Magic!* show. We were elated. The show was the 25th Anniversary edition at the Variety Arts Theater. The year was 1978. But, as the date of the show approached, we started to get a little concerned. We had lost communication with Moretti and only knew he would be staying with friends in Santa Ana on his arrival.

Then we got a call. It was Hans Moretti. It was pretty amazing because, in just a couple of years, Moretti could now speak English. Also his voice sounded a lot younger. Then we talked to his wife, Maureen, who explained this was not the father we had seen in Vienna. This was his son who also did the same act.

It was hard for us to believe that anyone could duplicate the effects of the older Moretti. It was a moment a producer has nightmares about. "But we booked Sinatra! Oh, it's not Frank, it's Sam?!" It was too late now. We had "the Moretti's" ... It just didn't happen to be the Moretti's we thought we had!

Then came the night of our preview performance. The Moretti's, now billed as "Pandar and Partner" were absolutely sensational. Moretti's son proved to be a younger clone of his father and all the magic was there! They have since become one of the most successful acts in the business spending most of their time in Reno and Las Vegas. Also they are very nice people. P.S. that show introduced a talented young magician comedian to the non-asphalt stage, Harry Anderson. He was our emcee for the evening. Wonder whatever happened to him?

Aubrey

One of Hollywood's finest cinematographers was James Crabe. He was an Emmy Winner, Oscar nominee, Clio Award winner. His films included such classics as *Rocky*, *The Karate Kid* and *Save the Tige*r. He had impressive film and TV credits. But the world of magic knew and respected Jimmy Crabe as "Aubrey, the Magician." In his youth he was an absolute master of his craft. His manipulation was second to none. His illusions were inventive and his showmanship superb. Aubrey made more appearances than any other illusionist on Art Baker's *You Asked for It* show. He gave up the idea of becoming a star in magic to pursue his other love, the camera. But he never lost his interest or his magical talent. Army Grant, Brother Bill and I brought Aubrey out of magical retirement several years ago for our ABC-TV Special *Like Magic*. He was sensational.

"Jimmy" Crabe was just my age. I was the star of the very first film he ever ran through a camera. I drove my 1949 MG-TC under a bridge and he shot the scene on his used 8mm camera. When he first got a 16mm camera I did a Chaplin-esque scene in the backyard of our family home Brookledge. He used 200 feet of B&W surplus film and the budget for the entire film, including the whipped cream pie, was under ten bucks! He developed the film in his basement and it looked very professional except for some light flashes. His "Pappy" Lyle, came into the darkroom basement and lit a match to see what his son was up to.

Chang

I started producing the *It's Magic!* stage shows in 1956. For three decades it was always a thrill to bring great legends of magic to the stage. We had the chance to see Harry Blackstone Sr., Jack Gwynne, John Calvert, The Great Virgil, MacDonald Birch, Richiardi and many other great names in magic.

In 1962, the year we were hammering and painting on a soon-to-be-opened Magic Castle®, I was particularly excited about the booking of "Chang, the Magician." Chang, like Fu Manchu and Tihany, was a superstar of magic in South America but had not been seen in the United States. Booking Chang was a giant achievement. He would be coming into the U.S.A. by way of Texas. He would be happy to do the show but it was up to us to procure the illusions and assistants for him. He could bring his costumes and small props but we had to stage the show.

We worked out a deal with the late Al Jansen, the son of Dante, the Magician. Chang would perform Dante's "Crushing a Woman Illusion" that was also a feature of Chang's illusion show. We hired the best magic assistants and eagerly awaited the arrival of the master magician.

I was set to pick up Chang at the airport but we got word that he would be arriving at the downtown Greyhound bus station from Dallas. I drove my pickup truck to the station and waited for the arrival of the great Chang. The bus unloaded the passengers but I didn't see Chang.

When all the people had left the waiting area, I looked around and noticed one old unshaven man sitting on a couple of cardboard boxes that looked like recycled homes for the homeless. In fact, he looked like one of those homeless winos of Main Street. Could this be my star? Could this be the seventh and last edition of *It's Magic!*? I approached the old man and said: "Chang?" He said: "Mr. Larsen?" Somehow I sensed I was in trouble. Chang stayed at the Dante ranch and went to work with the cast and crew.

The night the show opened, October 20, 1962, I was the only person in the audience that could appreciate the greatest magic effect ever seen. I saw the amazing transformation of an old man into a tall and perfectly groomed stage personality. Those boxes had contained change after change of gorgeous Chinese robes. His magic was flawless. His magnetic personally was amazing. Every movement was perfect. Chang was truly a great magician.

After the show Chang, the Magician vanished! I took an old unshaven man with a couple of old cardboard boxes back to the bus station. It was Chang's first and last appearance in Los Angeles.

Virgil the Great

The name Virgil Mulkay probably doesn't mean too much to the average person. But "The Great Virgil" was one of the finest magicians I have ever seen. Virgil was a schoolhouse magician. He played school auditoriums and civic theaters. Audiences that marveled at his performances on stage would have been equally amazed if they witnessed the greatest trick of all, packing one of the world's most spectacular illusion shows into one semi-truck.

Virgil and his wife, Julie, never stopped working. His show was legendary in the northwest and in foreign countries. In the history of magic, The Great Virgil earned and deserved the title of "The Great." Virgil and Julie took their show to the people. They played the sticks. They packed big auditoriums with a Broadway type show that never played Broadway.

A favorite recollection goes back to the early fifties when Virgil played his big show at the Wilshire Ebell Theater here in Los Angeles. Our Dad, Bill Larsen Sr., was seated at the back of the house with the legendary Dante. Dante leaned over to Dad and said, "Great show, Bill, but it's too small for the big towns and too big for the small towns."

I started producing *It's Magic!* at the same theater in 1957. Every year I was reminded of Virgil's appearance there. There was a big steel support pipe across the narrow alley at the Ebell, next to the stage door. It was high enough for the small trucks but too short for the big trucks. Bobby Fenton had driven Virgil's huge semi truck into that pipe. The accident left a pipe shaped dent in the front of the truck, and a truck shaped bend in the pipe!

Harlan Tarbell

For decades the old Philharmonic Auditorium in downtown Los Angeles housed the city's major musicals. It was the home of the Civic Light Opera. It was originally the Clune Auditorium and was built around the turn-of-the-century. It was the kind of a theatre where Klaw and Erlanger's *Ben Hur* was staged, complete with live horses. I remember seeing Judy Garland there in concert.

From my position in the uppermost gallery it was kind of like flying over Hollywood Park on the approach to LAX. As a teenager growing up in a magical family, the name Harlan Tarbell was simply a part of life. *The Tarbell Course in Magic* was the first correspondence course in magic. Later it was published as a hard bound course. In the late forties, Harlan Tarbell presented his one-man show at the gargantuan Philharmonic. Naturally, Brother Bill and I were there.

When the curtain opened the stage looked like a general store. Old tables were filled with magical props. The tables were probably stored in the basement—or maybe borrowed from the Salvation Army Thrift Store. The Legendary Tarbell entered looking like a cross between a school teacher and Harry S. Truman. The follow spot narrowed and this man started to talk and then he started to do magic. By the end of the evening that stage had been filled with more spectacle than all of Ben Hur's chariots. He performed little tricks for a huge theatre and the tricks became huge and the theatre became intimate. Now that's magic!

Alla Axiom

Brother Bill and I thrilled to the shows of Blackstone, Dante, Gwynne, Paco Miller, Virgil, and the other great traveling shows of the forties and fifties. Then there was ALLA AXIOM!

One day Dad was behind the counter of the Thayer Studio of Magic on La Brea. A dapper man came in and introduced himself as the advance man for the Alla Axiom Show that had been booked into the Wilshire Ebell Theater. He had some really nice posters and a bunch of impressive looking flyers. Dad was surprised that he wasn't familiar with the name Alla Axiom. The advance man explained that he seldom played the big metropolitan centers but his two-hour illusion show would bring a new ray of magical sunshine to the world. At that very moment, according to the advance man, this magical man of mystery was rehearsing behind closed doors at the Ebell with his entire company and his tons of equipment.

Dad put up the posters, promoted the show and waited for the big opening night. The advance man showed up from time to time to assure us that Alla Axiom would be the talk of Los Angeles. The big night came and we were all there in our complimentary seats. There was no orchestra. The overture sounded like a scratchy 78 r.p.m. record. That's because it was a scratchy 78 r.p.m. record! The Great Alla Axiom made his appearance from a puff of smoke. There he was—it was the advance man with a hokey stick-on goatee. Or should I say it was Alla Axiom who was his own advance man? His "company" was his wife. She had probably been a raving beauty a few decades back. Now she looked like she was smuggling walnuts under her tights.

The big illusion that closed the first half of the show was the classic "blade box." His wife laid down in the box and Alla Axiom did the whole routine with the blades. At the end he opened the box and tried to get his wife out of it. Axiom couldn't move her. She was stuck in the box! The curtain came down with the great magician still tugging at the poor lady. Dad was turning blue with laughter. He had to sit down on the curb in front of the theater of contain himself.

The second half featured the world's bumpiest Asra Levitation. This time he got Mrs. Axiom floating high off the floor but he couldn't get her down again. It was a great night. The theater manager said he hoped the next night's performance would be better. It was. Alla Axiom disappeared! The old heavy oak Asra mechanism was still in the Ebell basement up to a few years ago; a tribute to a man and his craft.

Dante! The Magician

I am often asked whom I consider the greatest magician I ever witnessed. There is no question ... Dante was the master. He was a dynamic personality who looked like a magician, talked like a magician and did absolutely amazing magic. He was probably better known in Europe than America but his world tours brought him to the United States often. We saw his full stage revue at the grand old Biltmore Theatre in downtown Los Angeles. It had a great dome from which he hung his triple trunk illusion.

His principal lady in the show was Moi-Yo Miller, who is an active member of the Magic Castle® and magically looks as glamorous as she did on the stages half a century ago.

Home base was always the Dante Ranch on Lassen Street in the desert now known as Van Nuys. As kids, we visited the ranch often. It had a private theatre, tennis courts, swimming pool, full woodwork and machine shop, a complete saloon and a huge warehouse where the props were stored.

One evening we visited the Dante Ranch and he introduced a young man from Denmark who had only been in the country a few days. Dante predicted a great future for his Danish friend. The young man did his comedy routine and devastated the audience. The young comic's name was Victor Borge!

The walls in the Dante room in the Castle are fascinating. Most of the panels are heralds from Dante's European tour of 1937-1938, including theatres like the Tivoli, Hippodrome, and Empire ... the biggest and best variety venues in the world. One of the illusions advertised was "Television Outdone—the transportation of a living person." Today you might not think too much about that but in the late thirties television was a dream of the future.

We got our first TV set in the late forties. We used to sit and watch the Paramount mountain—KTLA—with the news of the world running across the screen like a ticker-tape until about 6 p.m. when the real programming would start. Dante was clearly well ahead of his time with "Television Outdone," a combination of two modern cabinets with a scrim replacing the curtain. In Dante's hands, it was something akin to a miracle. The lady would fade away from one cabinet and fade into the other on the opposite side of the stage. Neat stuff in the pre-TV era.

Dante's show was a true magical stage revue; a spectacular and his illusions were presented as scenes. *Backstage with a Magician, Fountania, The Unsevilled Barber, Cabaret de la Morte*—each a masterpiece of magic. The walls in the Dante room are an education.

Dante ala Robert Harlan

Mark Wilson did his first *It's Magic!* at the Wilshire Ebell Theatre on November 6 & 7, 1964. Mark performed the entire second half of the show and he was great. At that time, Mark was starring in his own weekly *Magic Land of Allakazam* show on CBS-TV so it was quite a coup to have him on the show. Closing the first half of that show was an act that became one of the most unforgettable moments in the history of *It's Magic!* Bob "Torchy" Towner was a bright, young magician who billed himself as "The Great Rinaldi." Bob was a great admirer of Dante, the Magician and was a great friend of the Dante family.

Dante's son, Alvin Jansen, one of the original Academy of Magical Arts Board Members, gave Torchy permission to re-create the beautiful illusion scenes of all time, Dante's "Fountania" water fountain act. Al had all the original scenery, Chinese costumes, music and props. This is the act wherein the magician acts out a fantasy involving a stream of water from a small fountain. He picks up the stream with his finger and places it on the tip of his sword. He then causes it to multiply with a stream emanating from fans, wands, headdresses, until the whole stage was awash with sparkling ribbons of reflective water.

The climax to the act was when the magician gathered the water in half a coconut shell that he would hold over a scenic rock waterfall. Gallons of water seemingly gushed from nowhere creating a beautiful, foaming, cascading waterfall. Bill and I had seen Dante and Moi-Yo Miller perform this act at the old Los Angeles Biltmore Theatre. It was magical perfection.

Everything was perfect in Towner's re-creation of the spectacle—right up to the point of the gushing water from the coconut shell. I have to share a magician's secret with you. The effect worked through the modus operandi of a jet of water being deflected off the underside of the shell. The whole act worked on the principle of very precise controlling of the water pressure from a city water main. Al Jansen was controlling the

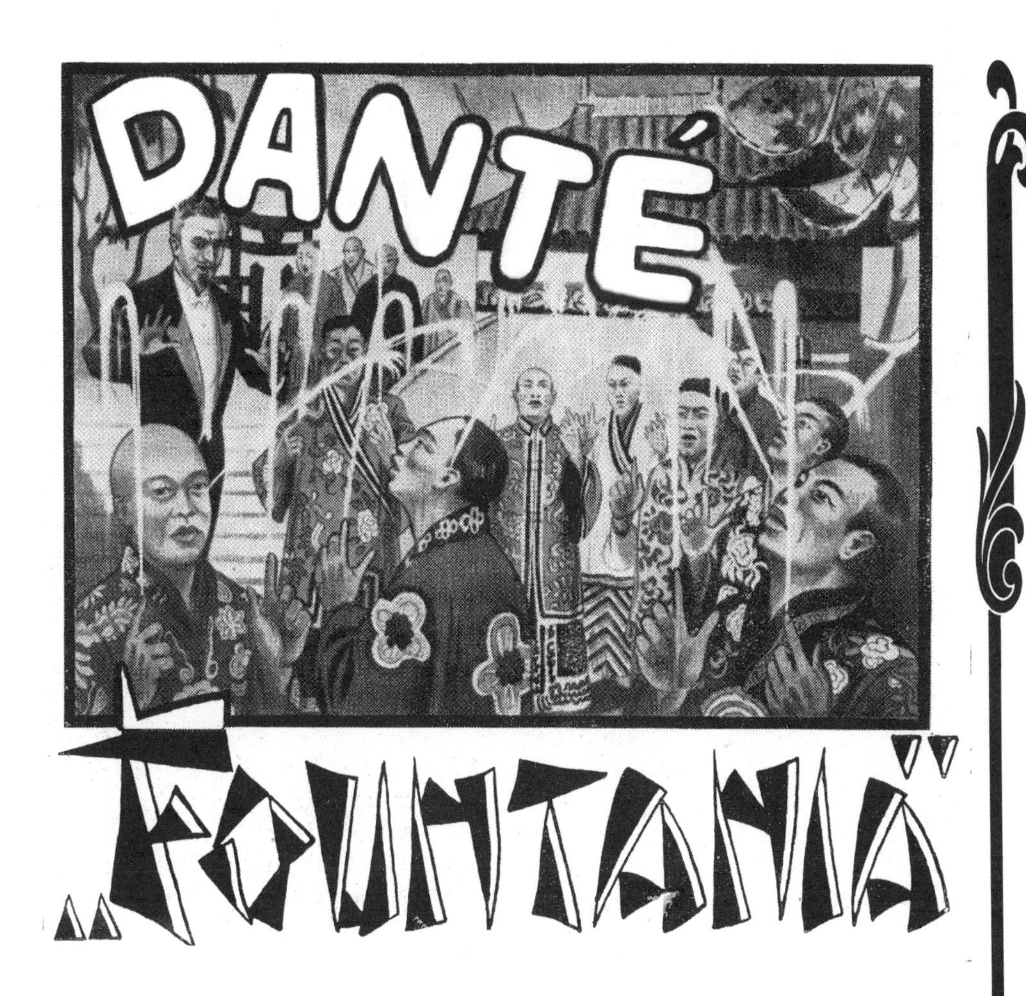

pressure when something went wrong. Torchy Towner valiantly tried to hold the water down with his shell. First one hand ... then both hands ... then, oops, no hands!

That jet of water shot into the air and we all know what happens when cold water hits hot light bulbs! The "Fountania" water act suddenly became a series of dazzling showering glass and popping footlight effects that would have made a rock concert of the 90's proud. The audience thought it was the funniest thing they had ever seen. "The Great Rinaldi" was devastated. Happily, the next night went perfectly. That was the year the producers bought two hundred-fifty dollars' worth of new light bulbs for the Wilshire Ebell Theatre.

David Copperfield and Dante's Chair

David Copperfield owns an amazing museum and library. This is the home of the John Mulholland Library, which probably would have been lost to the magic community if not for David's purchase of the entire collection. Less publicized was David's purchase of the Dante Collection that Phil Temple was selling under an arrangement with the Larsen family. When Ruth Hansen, Dante's daughter, sold the collection in the early seventies, a great deal of the material went to magician Lee Edwards. Bill and I bought the rest of the collection, mainly to help Ruth. At the same time we bought Dante's favorite chair; a rustic antique that Dante had at his ranch in the San Fernando Valley.

The chair brought back memories of our many visits to the ranch. When Irene and I saw that David had reassembled the entire Dante Collection, including the Phil Temple and Lee Edwards collections, Dante's top hat, his gold topped cane, etc., we both agreed that the chair should be in the Copperfield "Dante Museum." Many of our magician members erroneously believed that the chair had been donated by Ruth Hansen to the Academy. A few members complained that I had given David property that was owned by the Academy of Magical Arts. Not true. The chair was owned by the Larsen family and we gave it to David to add to his collection. I think Bill, Sr., Bill, Jr., Al and Ruth Jansen and Dante himself would have been happy with our decision.

Chapter Six

Shrum's Greatest Magic Trick

The Thomas O. Glover Sr. Annex

Some of our newer members may not know that the Thomas O. Glover, Sr. Annex (The Palace of Mystery, Parlour of Prestidigitation, Inner Circle, Peller Theatre, and the William Larsen Memorial Library) used to be a three-story parking garage. The story of how this all came to be goes back to June 1974. The Los Angeles Fire Department had been concerned over a few complaints of overcrowding at the Castle. The Castle had become such a popular club we simply didn't have enough room in our old former residence.

Our biggest showroom was what is now the little museum in the Haunted Wine Cellar. It held a very crowded 49 people. We did everything we could do to cooperate with the fire department, but let's face it, they were right! We had too little space and too many people!!!

Then, it was discovered we had been operating for eleven years under the wrong fire permit! One day a fire marshal visited with a very official order. They would post a marshal at the door and allow exactly forty-nine people in the building. Not in just the theatre, but in the entire building. That was our approved occupancy. Forty-nine!

To add to the dilemma, that evening we had a party booked for two hundred people ... a group of lawyers, no less. The time was about noon. The fire marshal was very sympathetic but "the law is the law" and he was there to make sure the fire department's order was upheld. Tom Glover called councilmen. Brother Bill called influential Castle members. I kept coming up with stupid alternatives like giving each guest a water-filled balloon and a pushpin. The clock was ticking and nobody laughed at my suggestions.

About three o'clock, the fire marshal came up with an idea. "You've got a type-I fireproof garage next door. Why not use it for your party?" He assured us that the garage could be used as a temporary showroom until we could figure out how to install fire sprinklers in the Castle. That was it!

Now, we had less than four hours to convert a parking structure into a nightclub. Our first guests were scheduled to arrive at 6 p.m. I made a call to John Shrum and got him out of a production meeting for the *Tonight Show*. "Got a small problem," I said. "We need an instant night-club ... like right now!" John said he was in a meeting but he'd do what he could.

The next couple of hours were real magic. Trucks started arriving from NBC with tons of scenery. There were two full bars from the old west sets and an old soda fountain. John sent over a canopy and a main entrance, paneled rooms, vinyl stage floors and Masonite floor decorations. More trucks appeared from Walter Allen's studio plant rental company (after all, Walter was a member and one of their biggest accounts was the Johnny Carson Show, thanks to John Shrum). John's fellow art director, Hub Braden, sent over a whole sound stage full of electrified Japanese lanterns and light fixtures. Bill called Marvyn Roy

(Mr. Electric) who happened to be staying at the Magic Hotel so we could have a great nightclub-style stage act. It was a miracle.

That night, we opened the doors at 6 p.m. with a fully operational Magic Castle® nightclub. We operated out of the garage for the next several weeks while fire sprinklers were installed in the main building. The Fire Department asked for a survey by the Building and Safety Department, who gave us a notice of seventy-seven items that needed immediate correction: wider doorways, more stairways. It was fun, but the novelty soon wore off and we started a two-seating-a-night policy allowing us 154 people a night under a temporary occupancy permit until the work was finished.

But good things come out of bad and that fateful experience gave us the idea of turning the parking structure into showrooms. Then we all agreed that the annex could be a permanent addition and work was started on connecting the kitchen and service area. When finished, it would make the idea a practical one. That's the story of our biggest and best magic effect: *The Garage to Club Trick.*

The area became the Tom Glover Showroom Annex and it's a great credit to Shrum's ingenuity. He made eight concrete pillars literally *disappear*. He combined old trash and new treasures and made a modern concrete shell look like a warm old club that has existed forever.

Ernie Evans helped find parts of old houses and buildings that were being torn down. All those bits and pieces of architectural relics found a home at the Magic Castle®. In 1988 the Los Angeles Cultural Heritage Commission placed The Magic Castle® on the list of Los Angeles Cultural Heritage Monuments, #195. The landmark status refers to the old Lane Mansion that is buried somewhere under all the antique treasures. The Castle is really a museum of old buildings, where every corner should have an historical plaque.

When we were building the new show annex next door, Ernie called and asked if we had any use for a couple hundred polished mahogany doors from an old hotel in Long Beach. I called John at NBC and asked the same question. The sandpaper voice graveled back: "You just found your paneling for the Palace of Mystery!" The next time you are in the showrooms, look at the walls. Chances are, you'll see holes where doorknobs used to be. A few of the old mahogany doors still have room numbers on them. (The amazing thing is that the doors were finished on both sides. So the plaster walls underneath have a nice view too!) The other night, we found a retired hotel house detective peeking through one of the door keyholes.

Two Years in the Making

The *Instant Castle Night* happened in June of 1974. The Palace of Mystery and the Tom Glover Showroom annex opened in June of 1976. What took so long? The job of building a showroom in the old garage area seemed pretty simple. After all, the building was there! Albeit, it was the structure designed to park automobiles. The floor levels of the garage were not at the same level as any floor in the Castle.

There was also the small matter of a forty-foot gap between the two buildings. This area would be filled with a two-story kitchen and service facility building that had to be designed and approved by the Building and Safety Department, now very aware of the existence of the Magic Castle®.

The entire project would cost about two hundred, fifty thousand dollars. The Glovers agreed to build the structure, including plumbing and electrical, but we were responsible for the decor, interior, air conditioning, trade fixtures, etc. We were not in the position to write out a fast check even though Brother Bill was at his best form getting the members to chip in contributions, advance dues, conversions to Life Members in addition to finding new members.

There was one other thing. If we were going to use the parking garage for showrooms, where do we park cars? Fortuitously, our landlord Thomas Glover had seen fit to buy the complex of bungalow apartments adjacent to the Castle on the east several years before. As the

IT WILL NOT
BE FINISHED
JAN 2ND FEB 1ST
MARCH 1ST. / APRIL FOOLS DAY!!
MAY BE SOME DAY?
¡MAÑANA MAÑANA MAÑANA!
FOR TRI-CENTENNIAL
WHAT ARE YOU BUILDING?
WATCH YOUR STEP

club became more successful, Tom agreed to tear down the twenty-six bungalows to make room for a surface parking lot for the Magic Castle®.

This didn't go over well with the people who lived there, even though they were all on a month-to-month rental agreement. Suddenly, we found ourselves in the middle of one of those highly publicized "breaking news" events. Neighbors and tenants were picketing the Castle claiming we were throwing poor unfortunates out on the streets and we were about to tear down a historic monument. (Tex Watson of the Manson murders had lived there.) The last tenant to go was a nice, old lady, her piano and her cat. You can imagine how much fun the media had with that one. In the meantime, the furor died down and the old apartment vanished like magic. The new parking lot literally paved the way (sorry about that) for the creation of our new showroom annex.

Taking everything into consideration, the years from inception to opening the annex were pretty damned amazing. During the construction many members and guests were never aware of the day and night building activities. In June of 1976 we celebrated the *instant* appearance of nearly six thousand square feet of space. That almost doubled the size of the original house. It was and is a proud accomplishment.

Don Damaskin

One of the carpenters was a rather amazing fellow who had just moved to Los Angeles from the state of Washington. He was a true "jack of all trades." Don was a carpenter, plumber, electrician, welder, artist, photographer, draftsman ... you name it. When the job was completed we kept this young man on our payroll. He became my technical right-hand-man.

Don Damaskin was in charge of all technical aspects of the Magic Castle® and that's one helluva bunch of aspects. He was our man behind the scenes from 1976 until his untimely passing in 1995. He also took on the challenge of our publishing department and it was because of Don that our newsletters had a new look. He had a vast understanding of the wonderful world of the Macintosh computer.

Larsen's Folly

When I first proposed the idea of turning the garage space underneath the Palace Theater into a theater, ballroom and library complex, everyone thought I had gone completely bonkers. The ceiling was too low, the area was full of posts and the only way to get there was down the service driveway and past the trash compactor. On the other hand, I argued, it was the perfect place to relocate our library that needed a new home. The old library was an intimate hideaway on the third floor of the old house. Although it was charming it had almost no security and no one even wanted to think about the potential loss in case of a fire. Fire sprinklers and rare books are enemies. The garage was the perfect answer. The steel and concrete construction built back into the hillside made it a veritable bomb shelter. It tripled the space for our book collections and even later provided a needed classroom.

The key to making the space practical was the enclosure of the existing outside fire escape stairway that was for emergency purposes only. The Fire Department was thrilled with the idea of bringing the stairway up to code by enclosing it. We were thrilled with the idea of making a really grand stairway that would lead to the lower level activities. Because of this added space, we have been able to increase revenues through private parties and meetings as well as giving the members the magician's library.

The Albert Peller Theater

Al Peller loved the Magic Castle®. It was literally his home away from home. He was one of those people who loved to entertain and who would happily do his show for anyone who would stop and watch him. Al passed away in 1989. His memory is perpetuated by the intimate Albert Peller Theater on the Inner Circle level. Thanks to generous donations by Mrs. Albert (Triny) Peller we were able to outfit this little theater with large screen projection TV facilities and it has been the popular home for corporate meetings and unscheduled magic performances. We are currently looking over plans for a new design for the Peller Theater that would make it into a fabulous magic showroom. The plan by art director Joe Hoffman would make this all purpose theater look like a private theater in a castle in Europe.

Watts Art Glass Windows

One day I got a call from a lady who had called about ten years earlier. She explained that she had some old art glass windows that she still wanted to sell. Ten years ago I told her we really didn't need any more windows. I think she called at a time when my warehouse was full and my pockets were empty. She said she still had the windows but the place where she had them stored was about to be torn down. Would I be interested? Again I explained that I really didn't need any more windows but curiosity got the better of me. Even though I had a heavy duty business lunch meeting at the Castle and a Friday lunch menu to knock off that Friday morning I made a date to meet the lady on a street corner in Watts.

Now Watts is a section of Los Angeles probably most famous for the Watts Riots, an area where a white kid in a Chrysler LeBaron convertible is not an every day sight. I was there right on time and met a very stylish and delightful lady. Everything on the block had been torn down except one old single car garage. She had a rather elderly helper with her who gingerly opened the old wooden garage door.

Inside there was a stack of glass panels. At a glance I could see they were not too interesting. It looked like just colored glass of the type that might have been used as a wall divider in an old restaurant. The other problem was the windows were stacked flat which is very hard on glass windows and the pigeons had been using the whole place as a bathroom for years. I asked what she wanted for the lot and she simply said that someone had told her they might be worth a lot of money. I answered that they might have a value to someone but that someone just wasn't me. She had mentioned that the little garage was scheduled to be bulldozed the next week so I whipped out the two neatly folded one hundred dollar bills I kept in my pocket for such occasions and offered her that for the stack of pigeon poop.

She said she had heard the Castle was a really nice place and thought the windows would be happier there than in a dumpster. Then I produced a neatly folded picture of General Grant and offered her helper the fifty bucks if he would deliver the whole mess to the Magic Castle. The deal was done. A week or so later an old pickup truck arrived with a load of something that sort of resembled glass. I asked our amigos to use our steam hose on them to clean them up. It wasn't until that time that I realized the twenty or so panels were really very beautiful and exactly what I had been looking for to create an interesting wall in the new Inner Circle Ballroom. To top it all off the stained glass art depicted wine, a minstrel and a wonderful Castle. It was almost as if the wall had been designed for the Castle. We lucked out again!

Castle Whodunits

Considering we've been around for over a quarter of a century, we've had relatively few problems with thefts. There have been a few, almost comical capers. Once we opened our offices on Monday morning to find the weekend receipts missing. In those early days, we didn't have a real safe so we kept the money in a strong box hidden away in a back room. The Hollywood police were called in. There was no break in. The theft had to be an inside job!

No one would have known the whereabouts of the loot except the owners, the management and the bartenders. (Bartenders always make the best suspects, next to butlers, of course. But we didn't have any of those.) Everyone agreed to take the lie detector test. One day I got a call from the Hollywood police detective handling the case. He asked if I would come down to see if I recognized a burglary suspect that had been working the neighborhood. I met the detective at the station but the suspect was a stranger to me. As the officer and I walked out of the old Hollywood police station together and I waved "Hi" to a passing pedestrian.

"Who was that?" the detective asked. I told him it was our bug man, a real nice, young guy that worked for the exterminator company. I got into my truck and drove away. When I got back to the Castle, I was told to call the detective. The Hollywood police had our burglar in custody. Can you believe the odds of our running into the bug man who just happened to be on his way to report to his parole officer? The very sharp detective had recognized him and simply put two and two together. He was the one non-employee who had access to the back rooms. He admitted to the theft. Nice kid ... tough luck!

Before we built the showroom annex, we had a little *Orchestrion Room* off Invisible Irma's Room. My Imhof Mukle Orchestrion would groan, honk and wheeze to the delight of the depraved few that enjoy such things. It operated at the drop of a coin into a large grail cabinet marked *offerings*, a brass plaque from a recently demolished church.

The glass door of the cabinet was faked up with about a foot of coins with a shelf of coins on top. The effect was that there were hundreds of coins in the box. Not true, but the old Imhof did take in a number of *offerings* every night. It was there for fun, not for profit. It was kind of fun watching the pile of coins grow, like a piggy bank.

Over a period of time, I noticed that the pile wasn't getting any higher. I started paying particular attention to the Orchestrion Room. It was still very popular every night. Could it be that people were using thinner coins? Invisible coins? The door to the cabinet was always locked. There was no evidence of anyone trying to break in. It was a mystery.

I started slyly marking coins. I'd check and the coins would be gone. It was real magic! It wasn't the money; it was the principle of the thing. Someone, somehow, was ripping off Mr. Imhof's hard-earned moolah. But how? It was driving me crazy! It was like having a pesky mouse around the house. It must be a phantom burglar. Maybe Invisible Irma had a crooked kin.

The Sony half-inch black and white video recorder had just come on the market and we had one of the first ones. How to catch a mouse? Set a trap. We rigged up the video camera to turn on any time the coin box door was opened. The trap worked like a charm. One morning, I checked the recorder and there it was! A beautiful scene of a young man kneeling down, looking around to make sure he was alone, pulling the loop out of the lock hasp, and skimming off the top layer of coins. Then he replaced the hasp, took one last look behind him ... right into the lens of the camera ... and left. The sneaky burglar turned out to be the brother-in-law assistant to our janitor at that time. Now we knew who it was, what do we do about it?

Our manager, George Bardossas had a great idea. I called John Schuyler, a towering 6'6" type, who had helped set the camera for the trap and asked him to come to the Castle the next morning. Then I called our magician/friend and County Deputy Sheriff, Jim Warner, and asked him to join the party.

The next morning, the janitors were there. I asked them if they liked television. I told them we had this great new privately recorded videotape. I invited a *couple of the guys* to watch it. "Take a coffee break, come on up and join the fun." Sensing it was a great porno break; they headed for the office. I introduced them to Big John and made sure Jim Warner flashed his ever-present service revolver under his jacket. Then we started the tape.

As the janitor watched his TV debut, we watched him visibly pale. It was like touching the bulb of a thermometer with an ice cube. We told him we now owned their janitor equipment and they had five minutes, not only to leave the building, but also to leave Hollywood. We were not going to have Sergeant Warner toss them in jail but the tape would go into our safe for future evidence. If they were ever seen in Hollywood again, they would be sent up for life! They left ... never to be seen again.

Herrmann's Coach Cup

"In the beginning, there was magic in the air. The magic of day and night, of winter and summer ..." Those words were written by John Northern Hilliard in his classic book: *Greater Magic*. When the Larsen family presented their lecture on the "cultural background of magic" our mother, Geri Larsen Jaffe, used that beautiful piece to open her part of the act. At one point in the lecture mother displayed a coach cup that had been given to her by the legendary magician "Silent Mora." The cup had been the property of Adelaide Herrmann who took over the Herrmann illusion show after Alexander Herrmann's death. The cup had been fashioned from a large Brazilian nut. It was rimmed with silver and had the name "Addie" engraved on it. We had it on display with some of our other magical treasures. The cup vanished many years ago along with some other priceless magical items.

One day mother, thinking the cup was still on display at the Castle, wanted to present it to James Hamilton whose act was a remarkable recreation of Herrmann the Great. She mentioned it to Jim and he was elated. Then we had to break the news that the rare piece of magical history had been borrowed.

Over the years we've had very little loss, pilferage or vandalism of our rare memorabilia. I have always liked to think that everyone admitted within these walls has a respect for the history of the building and its contents. The Magic Castle® is a place where the background of magic is cherished. It is a place where beautiful objects are shared by all visitors. But, we have lost a few precious items.

Sometimes a partying patron might think it is funny to take home a souvenir. Ed Saint's cat's eye cane is on the missing list. So is Houdini's original crystal ball. So is the silver cigarette lighter given to our father by Caryl S. Fleming soldered with fraternal pins from worldwide magic clubs. One day we unwrapped a package mailed to us and found a compete set of Castle silverware! Obviously someone had taken it as a prank and sobered up the next morning.

This is a long story but it has a happy ending. When James Hamilton was doing his act at the Castle the missing Herrmann coach cup mysteriously appeared in his dressing room. No explanation, it just magically appeared. It is now part of James Hamilton's collection per mother's wishes.

El Tinno

One time I wrote about a missing suit of armor in the Friday Gazette and mentioned it in an article in the Castle Newsletter. The saga started after the evening of Cinco de Mayo. Our big tin suit of armor gift from member Sam Pattissi was standing next to the kitchen door when I left the club about 1:30 in the morning on my way to my next door apartment. When I met our maintenance amigo Evaristo, later at 7:30 a.m., he asked what happened to El Grande el Tinno? Obviously, someone had stolen it. I wrote about the theft and posted a one hundred cash reward for the return of the thing. After a couple of weeks, we assumed it was probably history, likely sold for a few bucks at the local scrap yard.

Our General Manager at the time, Al Davis lived in Simi Valley and rarely visited his branch bank in Hollywood. A Simi Valley person seldom ventures further south than Franklin Avenue. One day Al made a rare visit to the Sunset/Vine branch. He returned to the Castle via Selma Avenue, which runs parallel to Hollywood Boulevard. Just as he was going past the hind end of El Capitan Theatre, he noticed half a suit of armor being loaded into a van. He stopped and met the owner of the van, a nice lady, Jani Oliart, who owns the Rocket Hollywood candy store next to the theatre. He explained that the armor was missing from the Magic Castle®.

She brought it back and here's the story: Her maintenance employees seldom work into the wee hours but two of them were working on the morning of May 6th. About 2:30 a.m. they heard a huge crash. They ran outside expecting to see a major car accident. Instead, they saw a pickup truck careening down Hollywood Blvd. and the legs of a tin man in the street. As the truck passed Highland, they heard another crash and saw the top half of the suit hit the pavement. The truck kept on going.

Her amigos hauled the two halves into the store, one of them retrieving the upper half from a block away! Nobody knew where it came from so, after a week or so, the owner of the store was going to take it to her ranch in northern California. She was delighted to give it back to us. I insisted that she accept the reward, which she gave to her two amigos.

Canopy Capers

The building of the Castle over the years proved that nothing, absolutely NOTHING went as planned. I suppose that's because I never really had a plan to begin with. We kind of invented things as we went along.

You may have wondered about the grand cast iron canopy over the main entrance to the Magic Castle®. We found it on an old lodge hall that was being demolished at the corner of Wilshire and La Brea. We moved it to the Castle where it sat in the parking lot driveway. Its only apparent value was in slowing down vehicles as they accidentally backed over its sharp, pointy ornamenture.

It was too heavy to hang from the front entrance of the mansion so we had to wait until we were doing some required foundation work in the basement. At that time, pilings were installed and four steel posts were put in place to support the canopy. Those posts are inside the wooden columns you see today.

Now came the tricky part. We rented a huge forklift to hoist the canopy into position. Everything was fine until the forklift, with canopy aloft, rolled up to the house. We had forgotten to tell anyone that the pavement in front of the door was actually part of an old porch and under that porch was part of the basement. The front wheels of the forklift suddenly became part of the basement!

The only thing that saved us from having a canopy where the wine cellar is now located was the fact that the 1908 house was built to withstand the blunders of mortal man and his machines. It was quite a sight, but that night our members used the old main entrance in the front of the house. The new *canopied* main entrance would have to wait for the tow truck in the morning!

James G. Williams

One day, a friend wanted me to meet a young Viet Nam Vet who had been entertaining troops and wanted to be a TV comedy writer. We made a date to have a cocktail hour meeting with the idea of explaining the hard facts of show business to his friend. I met James Gordon Williams and was impressed with his wit and exuberance but then I told him how hard, impossible, it was to get a foot in the door in the TV biz. I gave him the same advice that my mentor Snag Werris had given me. "If you want to be a TV writer, sit down every day and write something. Pretend you are working on a show and write a gag, a script, a story line, whatever. It might take years to get a job but that's how you do it." I wished him well with his career, apologized for not being more positive and helpful, and asked for a phone number "in case anything comes up."

The next day, Bobby Lauher and I were asked to write Vin Sculley's new NBC game show, *It Takes Two.* I said we'd do it if the producers would hire a third writer to do the research and "digging" which was necessary for that particular concept. The producer, Ralph Andrews, asked if I knew anybody. I said I had just met a talented guy who wanted a job. Ralph said to set up an appointment for the guy. The next day, James had the job. If our meeting with James had been days or months earlier or later, it would have been a different story. Sometimes you have to believe in the magic.

Working with James on *It Takes Two* also led to his writing for *Truth or Consequences*. James, Bobby Lauher and I produced and wrote a very funny, local show on KTLA-TV called *We'll Get You to Bed By Midnight Movie*. It featured the voices of June Foray and Daws Butler (of Bullwinkle fame) with a couple's point of view of two slippered feet in front of the TV set. It was a fun and crazy show.

I was (am) a beach bum. While others ate lunch I used to love to flake out on the beach, soaking up the rays. While we were building the Mayfair Music Hall in Santa Monica, the *beach break* was part of the way of life. James often joined me on the sand. When we would get to the proper napping place on the beach, I would always stick a little straw or twig in the sand. I told him it was the way I used to tell time.

Often he'd ask what time it was and I'd look at the stick and say, "It's five after two." He'd check his wristwatch and, sure enough, my twig was correct to the minute. This went on for many months. My electronics genius friend was really impressed by my simple and primitive way of creating a perfect sundial.

One day, it was overcast and there was no shadow. James was amazed that I could still tell him what time it was. I finally broke down and pointed out that clear view from the beach of the huge clock on the tower of the Crocker Bank building across the street from the Mayfair. So much for science!

Several days later, we were working on the Castle séance. James got even by putting Crazy glue on the top step of the ladder I was standing on. I think the shoes may still be attached. Funnnnnny!

Houdini Séance

The original idea of the Houdini Seance was to take William Larsen Sr.'s lecture on the Final Houdini Séance in 1926, add some mental mysteries and offer a scary, dark seance *ride*. Dr. Thomas Heric volunteered to take on the challenge of creating the electronics to run the séance. It was a marvel in step switches and relays and the machinery took up the better part of a room. It was fun just to watch the infernal beast at work, the machine, that is, not Dr. Tom.

The Mad Doctor and I worked on the effects and Ed "E. Raymond Carlyle" Fowler became our first medium. (Ed and I share the same birth date, the same day, and same year. Ed has made a career of being the world's most natural Santa Claus with his flowing white hair and beard. Born the same year? No way!) Ed was our "house medium" for years. Later he turned over his crystal ball to Sandy Spillman who, after quite a run, passed the ectoplasm to our current medium, Leo Kostka. Dr. Tom Heric also painted the portraits of Gilbert and Sullivan in the Irma Room and became my partner in the Mayfair Music Hall.

Dr. Tom passed the Houdini Séance soldering iron to James Gordon Williams, whose father, Gordon Williams, was responsible for such minor miracles as the Tiki Room and Abraham Lincoln at Disneyland. James, in addition to being a fine gag writer, was an electronics wizard and moved Harry Houdini into another world, a computer world. Thanks to James the room full of equipment now fits into a box about the size of a brick. James won an Emmy for his work as a sound technician. He still tends to Houdini's needs in creating that perfect place for Harry and Bessie Houdini to play.

The séance, which follows the multi-course gourmet-style dinner, is composed of two parts. Leo Kostka climbs into the minds of the ten guests and baffles them with feats of mental legerdemain. The finale of his show is the re-creation of the Final Houdini Séance that took place on the roof of the nearby Hollywood Knickerbocker Hotel in

1936. The guests join hands to form the mystic circle. The lights dim and the music begins. For the next ten minutes about thirty things *go bump in the night*. That's my department. One year ago James and I completely revamped the séance. It was a job that I thought would take about a week. Alas, it was a bigger undertaking than I thought and there were nights when Leo had to hope the real Houdini would make an appearance.

When I was hired as consultant for the multi-million dollar Caesar's Magical Empire at Caesar's Palace in Las Vegas, two lavish séance rooms were planned for the complex. I offered to show the engineers and designers from the Landmark Entertainment Group our séance. They had dinner and enjoyed the séance show. After the séance I joined the group and offered to show them the inner working of the séance. To my surprise the President of Landmark said they had seen enough. They loved the séance but the version they were designing for Caesar's would be much more sophisticated.

I was very proud of the séance and once again offered to show them the *machinery* that made it all work. They politely declined and departed. One of the team took me up on my offer of having a nightcap at the Grand Salon bar. I mentioned that I was disappointed that no one seemed interested in seeing the inner working of our accomplishment. He explained that they had already designed most of the effects and that some of them were already being made at a cost of something like $300,000. I think we dumped about $5,000 into our séance over the period of about twenty-five years!

Then he said that one thing we should be aware of should be to tell the guys in the black suits to be more careful. They had bumped into a couple of the guests seated at the table. I said we didn't have guys running around in black suits. During the séance the only one present in the room is Leo, the Medium with the guests. He winked at me knowingly and said: "Sure… sure…" Then we went back to finishing our drinks.

Without giving away too many of our secrets a number of the effects in the dark séance are motivated by Sears garage door openers. These amazing devices are built to raise and lower garage doors. Raising and lowering gags and gimmicks are nothing to these clever work horses. You have to be careful however. Once someone in the neighborhood got on our frequency. Every time they opened their garage door all hell broke loose in the séance.

It's always frustrating to spend a great deal of time and money on something no one will ever see. It's like the plumbing and electrical wiring in a new house. I always thought it would be nice to build a home with transparent walls so people could appreciate where the money went. An effect in the séance may only last five seconds but it represents months of invention, weeks of construction and hours of installation.

Yale Gracey

We were cleaning out one of our storage areas about a year ago and we ran across a big plywood box. It had been there for years and someone remembered that it had been pushed from storeroom to storeroom for years before that. When we got it out in the open, it turned out to be one of our most valuable museum items. I took it up to my shop in Santa Barbara and worked on it from time to time. Then James Williams and I installed it in the Inner Circle Museum area.

What is this mysterious box, you may ask? It is the original miniature working model of the "Pepper's Ghost" illusion that member Yale Gracey made for Walt Disney's Haunted Mansion. Believe it or not, Yale worked out the principle of the illusion before he knew about the magical effect, which goes back about one hundred years. James Williams' father, Gordon Williams, was one of those technical brains at WED and was a pioneer in animatronics. He made stuffed birds come sing and gave life to Abe Lincoln. He was a good friend of Yale Gracey who, tragically, was killed during a robbery at his beach home.

Gimmicks & Gags

The Alibi Machine

Over the years, we've had a bunch of crazy gimmicks at the Castle. They range from Invisible Irma to the Alibi Machine in the men's room, and our moderately obscene statue of David in the ladies' room.

James G. Williams and I came up with the idea for the Alibi Machine in the men's room. It is the machine that plays background sound effects next to the pay telephone. To show how long the machine has been around, the office background sounds are typewriters! Clickity, click, click–ding!

James is constantly working on the gimmicks in the Castle as a labor of love and a love for madness.

Sinking Stool

The sinking stool was the brainchild of member Floyd Baldwin. He thought it would be fun to have one bar stool that would imperceptibly sink into the floor. It was a really great idea so he built it and it worked fine. In its earlier form, the bartender would get the *pigeon* seated and then go into the back storeroom where he would release a valve that started the lowering action on a hydraulic piston attached to the chair seat. After the gag, the bartender had to go back and pump it up with a hand lever. The patron loved the gag but the bartenders hated it. Later, we changed it to an electric hydraulic pump and the bartenders started liking the idea ... especially when their tips increased.

The original sinking stool was at the end of the bar next to the stairs. Then we changed it to the other end of the bar that was, at that time, only half as long as the bar is today. Then we extended the bar so the sinking stool was in the middle of the bar. A few years later we moved the stool to its present location, the second seat from the end.

One day Bill and I had a cocktail hour appointment with a very well known writer who was doing a piece on the Castle for a national magazine. We had never met the gentleman who came in right on time for our appointment. Bill was finishing some business in the office and asked me to go downstairs to meet the man and have a drink or two until he could join us. I met the writer and we had a seat at the center of the bar, in fact, he sat on the seat where the sinking stool had been for years.

I found the writer fascinating and we found we had the same tastes in martinis. Shortly, Bill came down the stairs and sat next to the man at the bar. "Hi, Milt, sorry to be late, who's your short friend?"

Suddenly Bill realized what he had done. He had assumed the stool had sunk and he had come in on the end of the gag. In fact, this was a real bar stool. The gag one was in its new position at the end of the bar. The writer was a sadly deformed dwarf. He laughed and appreciated the situation as Bill tried to explain.

David's Soap

When we expanded the main floor men's and ladies rooms in the sixties, we added a few new gimmick touches. One was the statue of David in the ladies room. This was a really fun, if in somewhat questionable taste, little gag. It was a soap dispenser. To make it work, you simply pushed a button imbedded in David's navel. The liquid soap would then pump out of his penis. The ladies got a big kick out of it. We found there was a small problem however. When a man pushes a button to eject soap from a dispenser, he holds his hand under the spigot, no matter what it looks like. When a lady pushes the button she stands back to see what happens.

What happened? The soap would splash on the floor meaning the next occupant of the ladies room had a pretty good chance of slipping and sliding. In trying to solve the problem we redesigned David's *faucet,* which resulted in a large appendage (delighting some ladies while offending others.) We are constantly working on this project with the hope of one day reaching absolute perfection.

Revolving Table

This is a nice, simple gimmick consisting of nothing more than a round table top connected by a steel shaft to a very, slow geared-down motor below the floor. It should be fairly maintenance free except, of course, for those occasional guests who think it's fun to try to stop it forcibly or pretend they are driving a Greyhound bus using the tabletop as a steering wheel. To paraphrase: "Kids don't break adult toys ... adults do."

Traveling Glass

James G. Williams and I created a really fascinating little illusion that amused members and their guests for many years. At the time, we discontinued it because the bartenders felt it hampered their activities. We found out later the main activity the bartender was doing was stealing and that led to the dismissal of that particular individual. At this writing, James is working on installing a new version of our effect.

The gag was simply a traveling glass on the bar. The bartender could make a drink at one end of the bar and then the glass would travel down to wherever the customer was sitting. It worked on an ingenious principle and it was a fun, little gag.

Elevator's Ups and Downs

When the Castle first opened on January 2, 1963, all the activities were on the first floor. The dining room opened about a year later. In the old Lane home, the mezzanine area at the top of the stairs was known as an *orchestra promenade.* Those clever Victorians figured out that, by putting a deck in that position, one orchestra could play for guests on two floors. When the old mansion was turned into a boarding house during World War II, the mezzanine had been walled off as a small apartment. It was an exciting day when we tore off the plasterboard and found the original beautiful golden oak woodwork still intact.

The mezzanine made a nice place for a close-up table. It also made a nice place to hang two Gothic iron chandeliers that once graced a church at Adams and Vermont. We installed the grillwork from the elevator of the old Frontenac Hotel that used to perch atop Bunker Hill near the top of Angel's Flight Railway. This was to disguise a *secret* back stairway to the magicians' only library that was then in one of the former servant's quarters on the third floor.

The elevator became a strange and popular *gimmick* for the members and their guests. Upon pushing the elevator button, a monster face would appear in the blackness of the shaft. The eyes of the monster seemed almost lifelike. You could move your hand in front of the face and the eyes would follow the movement. After a minute or so of this interesting mechanical effect, the monster would lunge and shake the bars of the elevator grillwork. It sounds silly, but it scared the hell out of the customers.

The joys of management decreed that Brother Bill or I would usually play the part of the monster. This meant running up the back service stairway, donning the monster mask and doing the bit. It also meant ducking under a beam in the middle of the stairwell, which had been abandoned many years earlier. One day Bill forgot to duck! Brother Bill had a scar on his forehead to commemorate the event. As the Castle grew bigger and more popular, the monster gag had to be eliminated. When the monster lunged, drinks would fly and an occasional customer would also fly … down the stairs. To quote Queen Victoria, the insurance company "was not amused!"

Dropping Dora

A non-life-threatening gag was needed for the elevator, a new gimmick. I invented the ultimate special effect: "Dropping Dora!" By pushing the elevator call button you would start the action. A scream was heard. A scantily clad woman in a bloody negligee plummeted down the elevator shaft before your very eyes.

It was more complicated than it looked. A track extended from the attic to the basement– a run of four floors. The heavy plaster mannequin had to "free fall" down this track to look real. It was held at the top by a solenoid latch. A push of a button would disengage the latch. After the fall, the plaster mannequin had to latch onto a sprocket chain that would pull it back to the top. A black curtain hid the return trip and everything worked perfectly–until one night!

That night Dora made her final plunge. When the mannequin got to the bottom, it latched on the chain but, when it got up to the cage, the curtain caught on the rising figure, ripped it away and carried it to the top of the track. Because of the curtain, the mechanism failed to stop which jammed Dora's head into the plaster ceiling and broke the figure off the track! Now, the mannequin and the heavy curtain were much heavier than the counterweights so it plunged down the shaft without the guidance of the track.

When Dora crashed into the basement, the legs broke off the body and she lost the curtain. This made her lighter than the counterweights so the figure shot back up to the attic where it broke off its cables, broke away more plaster and the descending debris made one last trip down to the basement in front of the eyes of a fascinated audience. That was the end of Dropping Dora but not the end of the story.

About a year later, a laborer was shoveling the amassed silt of a half-century from the basement to make room for our Haunted Wine Cellar. You guessed it. His shovel came upon the half-buried, broken and bloody remains of Dropping Dora. The workman never stopped running … even long enough to pick up his paycheck!

Gory Head-A Really Bad Idea!

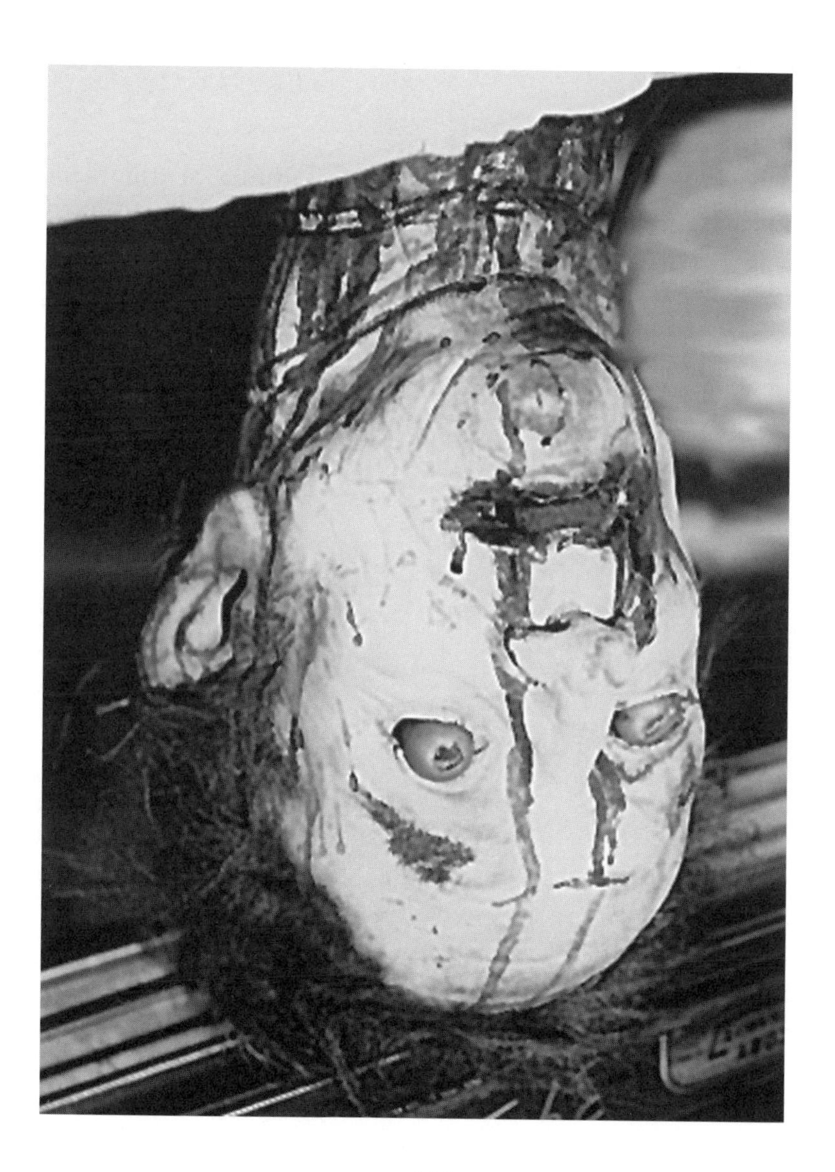

There have been a few blunders along the way. One particularly dismal failure was one of my best-constructed gags. The effect was simple. As the unwary patron walked down a hallway, a cabinet door, at eye-level, was encountered. The door had a sign on it that read: "Please do not open this door!" Naturally, everyone opened the door.

Inside, all that could be seen was the top of a man's head, as if the face-up body was lying prone with the feet away from the viewer. When the door was fully opened, it triggered the release of a meat cleaver which fell, neatly severing the man's neck and causing his head to fall with the face upside-down, and a look of horror in his eyes. The head was one of Verne Langdon's better efforts. The thing that made it really horrible was the fact that thick blood oozed from the severed arteries. It was really sickening!

I was very proud of the device. It worked without the aid of motors or pumps. It was all mechanical and very ingenious. The problem was the effect was too good. You need to remember that this was back in the sixties, before the days of *Freddie* and bloody chain saws. People going to, or coming from, dinner failed to see the humor in the gory head. We received so many complaints; I finally gave my bloody corpse a decent burial.

Castle Personalities

Dai Vernon, "The Professor"

Dai Vernon was considered one of the all-time greats in magic. He was a mere seventy-four years old when he came to Hollywood to visit Jay Ose in 1963. On that visit, he liked what he saw and started making plans to make the Magic Castle® his permanent home. For the first few months, Dai stayed with Jay in his room at the Castle. Later Bill Larsen offered to pay the rent on an apartment next to the Castle in exchange for occasional Castle lectures and *Genii* columns. For the next three decades Dai would be the *guest* of *Genii* and the Academy of Magical Arts. Bill wisely knew the value of having people like Harry Blackstone, Sr. and Dai Vernon *hanging around* the Castle.

Here's a quote from a *Genii* Magazine article that appeared in the April, 1993 issue. "Last month we had the pleasure of witnessing 'The Professor' at work as he presented his lecture-demonstration for the members of the Academy. Everything we had heard about this man was true, and after the lecture the members were torn on whether to take lessons from Dai and really become magicians, or to give up magic completely and go into glass blowing or less difficult hobbies. After watching Dai for two hours, the best magicians will realize how little he knows compared with his man. Every move he makes has a reason for it. Every sleight has been well thought out, worked on, reworked, and polished to the point that the sleights are unseen. Great skill goes almost unnoticed because the moves are so natural. I bow to one of our great close-up magicians and a fine teacher."

Dai Vernon was a fixture at the Magic Castle®. He could usually be found at the small round table at the Castle entrance with an unlit cigar and a snifter of brandy. He was always friendly, cordial and helpful to all magicians. Unless, of course, you were doing bad magic!

Larry Jennings

Larry Jennings became another legend in the field of close-up magic. He was a master card technician and a true innovator in the art. Larry was a plumber by profession before he turned his talents to full-time writing and performing magic. In the Castle's early days, Jay Ose was our Resident Magician but Larry Jennings was our *resident plumber*. Larry was a large man with hands that were those of a working plumber rather than the typical magician. This made his handling of cards even more remarkable.

In the late 60's, I was working in the shop when Larry Jennings burst in. He was frantic and wanted a crow bar. Why? Vernon's dead! Dai lived in an apartment next to the Castle. I tried to calm Larry down, grabbed some tools and we hurried over to the apartment. Larry banged on the door. He kicked and yelled loud enough to wake the neighborhood. There was no response. I peeked through the little *go-to-hell* window in his front door. My God! Larry was right! There on the bed was the lifeless form of the Professor.

By now Larry had ripped through the metal screen and the steel frame of the window. Larry was a big man but he crawled in the window and fell over a lamp and a table. Just as he reached the bed I heard a voice. "Hey, can't a guy get some sleep in here!" Dai was alive, well, and went on to live another couple of decades! Larry got busy repairing the damage to the apartment.

"Senator" Crandall

Probably the most colorful host the Castle has ever had was "Senator" Clarke Crandall. The Senator wasn't a Senator but he sported an almost Salvadore Dali waxed mustache and always smoked rum-soaked crooked cigars. That, plus the way he dressed, made him look something like a Senator from the deep south; deep south Chicago, as in Cicero. When Crandall greeted you at the front door you had the immediate feeling that you were probably not going to make it through our secret door. He talked down to members and guests alike calling them children and many a lovely lady would get a lecherous leer from The Senator.

How could this man be a host, manager, greeter? Everyone loved Clarke Crandall. He was a total character and he played his part beautifully. The Senator was also one of the most respected magicians in the world and his act was both pure magic and pure comedy. He liked to do his "X"rated midnight show, which was mighty tame by today's standards. In the seventies some of his material was a little on the *blue* side.

Don Lawton

Another very gregarious host/manager was Don Lawton. Don came to us from the mid-west and made his reputation in magic doing some of the corniest material ever written. Don met and married our first full-time receptionist Joanie Freiden.

One night Bill and Irene invited me over to the Brookledge for one of their frequent backyard barbeques. Don Lawton was one of the guests and after dinner he kept us in stitches with one joke after another. Then he admitted that he had gone to the trouble of memorizing dozens of jokes from our old Red Baker and Milt Larsen joke books. He just wanted to see how long it would take for me to recognize the material. I never realized our stuff was that funny.

Robert Stull

Bob Stull was a truly remarkable gentleman. At one time he owned and operated the Golden Gate Magic Company in San Francisco. He invented the famous effects The Stull Watch, The Stull Cigarette Dropper and the Stull Fish Bowl. He was the first person to ever do a commercial on radio and, as a Commander in the Navy, was instrumental in the development of radar during World War II. Many of the handcuffs in the Houdini Séance Room came from Bob's extensive collection of restraining devices. One of the props on display in the Castle is his wine barrel escape. Our mother, Geraldine Larsen used to love to tell of the time she was helping Bob at a magician's convention in Oakland, California. The barrel trick was brand new then and Bob had promoted it from a local winery. The barrel was so new; in fact, it still had a residue of wine on the inside. Mother was locked in the barrel as Bob did the trick outside on a hot summer day. By the time she escaped from the trunk she was half-looped from the alcohol fumes.

The barrel is an amazing prop. Through the use of a *gimmick* the barrel's top can be opened from the inside. Bob told us exactly where the gimmick was and exactly how to operate the barrel. Four of us tried to make it work and we spent hours trying to open it on several occasions. Finally we all gave up and asked Bob to come over and open it for us. He reached in, felt around for a couple of seconds and suddenly the latch opened. What's so unusual about that? At the time Bob was in his nineties and totally blind!

Charlie Miller

Charlie Miller was one of the greatest close-up minds in magic. He was a charming man who loved to work cruise ships where he could not only entertain with his magic but also dance with the ladies. Ap-

parently he was a superb dancer. Magicians were always a little envious when they would see Charlie and I having long chats at the Castle bar. They were sure Charlie was imparting fabulous secrets and magical methodology. The truth of the matter is that Charlie absolutely loved to talk about vaudeville and vaudevillians. He had been an acrobat in his early days and had an amazing memory of obscure novelty and comedy acts. He was a gold mine of information. Late in his life the rotund Charlie could still demonstrate some of the greatest pratfalls I have ever seen.

Bobby Lauher and I had the pleasure of writing for a TV show called *It Takes Two*, hosted by the famed sportscaster Vin Scully. Vin used to love to go to lunch with us. Once one of the crew asked Vin why he always went to lunch with the writers. Did we give him jokes and special ad-libs? Vin replied that both Bobby and I had absolutely no interest in baseball. We both thought a bat was something that hung upside down in a cave and a ball was an event where people danced. Apparently everywhere he went people would talk about baseball. Lunching with Bobby and myself was something of a vacation for him.

Peter Pit

A number of magicians who came to Los Angeles to perform in our *It's Magic!* shows in the early sixties, discovered the Magic Castle® and moved here permanently. Billy McComb, Shimada and Peter Pit became Castle fixtures.

Magician Whit Hadyn donated some wonderful Johnny Platt memorabilia along with a great story about Peter Pit. Peter was a member of the Academy Board of Directors for about twenty years and, as the club's secretary, Bill regarded him as his *right-hand-man*. Peter also helped Bill with the talent booking at the Castle and he produced and wrote many of the Academy awards banquet shows with Richard Zimmerman. He was a great emcee since he spoke about a dozen languages fluently.

Johnny Platt was a colorful figure at the Castle in his later years, always performing in an Egyptian robe and a red fez. Platt had achieved fame in the 30's with his version of the Hindu Rope Trick. He had a short section of rope that he kept as a souvenir of that illusion. Whit had admired the rope and John said that he could have it when he died.

When Johnny passed away, Peter Pit was executor of his estate and got all of Johnny's personal possessions and effects. From time to time Whit would ask Peter about the rope and Peter would always be a little evasive about it. As time passed, Whit kept reminding Peter about the fact that Johnny had wanted him to have the rope.

One day Peter met Whit at the Castle with a large box. Whit opened the box to find Johnny's Egyptian robe and fez. Peter spoke all those languages but had translated *rope* into *robe*! Whit donated the robe and fez to the Castle museum archives. We assume somewhere there is an old piece of rope waiting to be discovered.

Shull
Luck
Slydini
Dec. 7-49

Tony Slydini

One of the great legends of magic was Tony Slydini. Tony was an excellent stage performer as well as being one of the great teachers in close-up magic. He appeared on our 13th annual *It's Magic!* at the Wilshire Ebell Theater in 1967. When he was booked in the Close-up Gallery for the first time, he came to me and said he couldn't work the room. He said the large round table wouldn't work for his style of magic. I asked him what sort of table would work for him and he drew a half-circle on a piece of paper and handed it to me. I told him to come back in thirty minutes.

I grabbed my trusty Skilsaw and cut off the backside of the table. When Tony returned there was his table just like he had drawn it. Tony was delighted and impressed. The other magicians also liked Tony's design and the unusual half-round table became the standard table for all the magicians in the Close-up Gallery.

Monster Members

Almost all the famous monsters of the movies were either members or here as guests of members. Vincent Price loved the club. When he made the *Witchcraft Magic* LP for Capitol Records he insisted that the double cover would show the evil Mr. Rice peering out of our Open Sesame entrance door. Boris Karloff enjoyed coming in with his old friend Ralph

Edwards. Verne Langdon and I had the pleasure of producing another LP *Boris Karloff and his Friends* for Decca Records. What a talented and delightful man!

John Carradine was a frequent visitor to the Castle and his son, David, is still a member. Claude Raines was a good friend of Joan Blondell and loved to watch our first resident magician Jay Ose. Lou Derman once quipped that he loved doing the "Invisible Deck" for the Invisible Man. Lon Chaney Jr. said the Magic Castle® was the only place he really felt comfortable during a full moon. Cassandra Peterson is a friend of the Castle's and even lent us the use of Elvira's pinball machine for some time.

Bela Lugosi came in one night to find that we had a life-size figure of him seated in the Palace of Mystery box seat. Up to then I had never thought of Dracula breaking into laughter.

Johnny Carson

Johnny, Orson & Arthur

Arthur Godfrey

Arthur Godfrey was one of radio's biggest stars. His audience was not only huge but tremendously loyal. His down-to-earth folksy personality made people trust what he said. If Arthur told you something was good, IT WAS GOOD! It was as simple as that. Godfrey visited the Castle one evening as a guest of the legendary radio comedian Henry Morgan, who was a member and, although he lived in New York, was a frequent visitor to the Castle.

The next thing we knew, Arthur was back in New York extolling the virtues of the Magic Castle® on his CBS show. He told of the wonderful atmosphere, the great food, the celebrities that he met, and the thrill of seeing magic as it should be done. He ended by telling his audience that, if they were ever in Hollywood, they absolutely had to visit this wonderful place. It was a fabulous plug but there was a problem. At no time did he mention that the Castle was a private club.

He was barely off the air when the telephone started ringing—and they kept ringing! It was more than our small switchboard could handle. Bill telephoned Godfrey's offices in New York and, to his surprise, talked directly to Arthur Godfrey himself. He was chagrined and explained that he was there as a guest and no one had mentioned to him that it was a private club. He told Bill not to worry—he would let his audience know it was a private club.

True to his word, his audience of millions heard Arthur repeat all the wonderful things he had said the previous broadcast, and then he went one further to say that the Magic Castle® was a private club. You can't just walk in. You absolutely have to be a member. Then he topped it off by saying he was there because he was a guest of a member. So he said to go find a member and let them take you there, or become a member. And then ... why don't you call my good buddy, the President of the club, Bill Larsen in L.A. —Where there's a Bill, there's a way! Of course the phones started ringing again. Arthur had found his way to become a member and came in frequently when he was in town.

Orson Welles

Orson was a great lover of magic and a really wonderful magician. As a kid I remember seeing his Mercury Wonder Show in a tent in Hollywood. It was presented for the service men of World War II and his assistants were Rita Hayworth, Joseph Cotton and Marlene Dietrich. Dad had provided a number of the illusions from Thayers Studio of Magic so we caught the show several times. Here was a great star of the movies having the time of his life performing magic.

During the run of the show, Orson needed a prop and the Thayer Studio wasn't open. He broke a window, opened the door and helped himself. When Dad got home there was a note from Orson Welles. "Dear Bill, Sorry about the window ... triple the cost and send me the bill. Orson"

Once Orson hosted a magic documentary from the Magic Castle®. Unfortunately, Orson was in Europe on the dates they set for shooting the Castle scenes. No problem, they would use a double and shoot around him. Orson could come in later to shoot the matching shot introductions. Then the producers found they had a problem. During his trip to Europe Orson had gained about one hundred pounds! Due to a fairly low budget the producers worked with what they had. Viewers saw the back of Orson Welles entering our Open Sesame door. Then they saw Orson walking into the Grand Salon, obviously a much bigger man.

Johnny Carson

Johnny started his show business career as a magician and ventriloquist. One of my favorite bits in our Variety Arts archives is a takeoff that Johnny Carson did on his 1955 CBS-TV show that preceded the *Tonight Show*. Johnny was reading the mind of an audience member, ala Dunninger. Joseph Dunninger made his debut in 1941 on network radio and was a spectacular success. For those of you too young to remember Dunninger, he was a mentalist that astounded radio audiences with his ability to read minds over the airwaves. In Johnny's version he had an obviously nervous guy stand up in the audience and revealed many personal facts about him ... including the fact that the man is a notorious spy!

Joe Dunninger was married to Crystal Spencer, one of the most beautiful showgirls of the Ziegfeld Follies. There is a great tinted photo of Crystal Dunninger on the right in the art gallery hallway on the way to the showrooms.

Johnny has always loved magic and presented magicians whenever he had the chance on his legendary NBC *Tonight Show*. Discarded scenery from the *Tonight Show* would often find its way to the Magic Castle® thanks to the conniving designs of Johnny's Art Director, John Shrum. Shrum was very honest about his intentions. Johnny and producer Fred DeCordova always knew they were contributing to John's *standing set*.

Orson and Johnny

One night Johnny's guest was Orson Welles. Naturally the conversation led to their mutual interest in magic. In the course of the interview, they mentioned they were running out of time but they would get together after the show at the Magic Castle®.

After the show Orson and Johnny showed up at the Castle and had a nice time enjoying the performances of eager magicians and, in turn, showing the magicians a few new sleights. They spent a couple of hours and then left about midnight.

Many people don't realize that the *Tonight Show* is taped early on the West Coast for East Coast viewing. By the time our West Coast viewers watched the show Johnny and Orson had come and gone. The minute the show was over the phone started ringing and our driveway became a traffic jam of people who just happened to think of dropping by for a *night cap*. By the way ... "Wheeerrrrree's Johnny!"

Johnny & John

John Shrum was a very modest and retiring type of person. He was amazingly camera shy and there are very few photos of him in this book to attest to that fact. He was a large and imposing man and his trademark in the halls of the NBC Burbank studios was that he would always wear a suit with very flamboyant vests and a matching bow tie. On weekends or when working on construction projects around the Castle he would dress in a one piece jump suit and carry a live parrot, Ditto, on his shoulder.

Although I met John when he was an art director on the *Truth or Consequences* show, he became the art director of *The Tonight Show* starring Johnny Carson when Johnny moved from the east coast in the mid-sixties. John designed all the sets for Johnny until his sudden passing in 1988.

There was never an end-of-the-season wrap party because *The Tonight Show* went on and on fifty-two weeks a year. Every year, however, Johnny and producer Freddie DeCordova threw a thank you party for his staff and crew. The yearly party would usually feature hi-jinks with non-performer staff members doing crazy bits. John Shrum, modest man that he was, always avoided doing anything in the spotlight. His job was to create settings in which people would look good … not to be part of those settings. He steadfastly said no when asked to be part of the show.

One night we met at the owl bar. John's seat is the barstool at the extreme right of the mezzanine bar. It is marked with a brass plate in his memory—the inscription reads: "John Shrum 1927-1988—May he rest in bitters." John's favorite drink was an "old fashioned," Bourbon and a dash of Angostura Bitters always with a garnish of an orange slice. John said he had a problem. His fellow workers were really pressing him to do some kind of an act at Johnny's year-end party. Maybe he could do a magic trick. I mentioned a couple of box tricks that would pretty much work themselves but he panicked at the thought of doing anything that might have needed acting ability, talent or rehearsal. I came up with the idea of re-creating one of the great novelty acts of all time – "Le Petomane."

Le Petomane was a real performer, Joseph Pujol, who lived from 1857 to 1945. His act consisted of the controlled passing of gas from his intestines. It was, believe it or not, a class act. Le Petomane could blow out candles, cause objects to move, and do other wonders using his unique skill. He gave up the act after World War I. Remarkably he lived to be almost 90 before his passing. I prefer to think he just ran out of gas. There is a book about this performer in our library for those who think I'm always kidding.

Once the Le Petomane idea was hatched the NBC special effects prop guys and the wardrobe people went to work. John's Victorian tail suit was modified to accommodate a modest plastic fake derriere to be exposed. All John had to remember to do was: 1. Walk on the stage center. 2. Bow to the left. 3. Bow to the right, etc. We would do the rest.

Thanks to the genius of the prop makers John apparently blew out a candle and then a whole candelabra of candles. He caused small windmills to spin on the amply padded breasts of the beautiful Linda Nichols and pretty much caused a hurricane on the set each time he bent over. Needless to say it was hilarious and John left the stage to a gale of laughter and applause. Did this moment in the spotlight mean John would be bitten by the performing bug? He said it was the worst moments of his life and told me what I could do with Le Petomane and his candles.

Standing Sets

The Castle has been seen in hundreds of TV shows and theatrical films. John Shrum always called the Castle his best *standing set*. John also designed our Variety Arts Center and the Mayfair Music Hall. When they filmed the TV movie on the life of Mae West almost all the scenes were shot at one of the three locations. John kidded that he designed all the sets and some other art director got all the credit.

I've been in TV most of my life but I'll never understand some of the thinking. When a production company is scouting a location it will usually start with someone with a camera that looks at various rooms. If there is interest, the next step is usually a small army of tech folks who check it out. Then the big day arrives and the technicians, camera folks, producers, directors and actors appear to shoot the scenes. The Castle has doubled as a haunted house, a bordello, a posh hotel and, of course, quite often a place where magicians perform.

Once that whole parade took place with a commercial production company choosing the main bar as the perfect spot to shoot a commercial for Del Monte Foods. The day of the shoot came and the set dressers swarmed in with yards of fabric and some props. When they were done you could see absolutely nothing of our grand old Victorian bar. They could have easily shot the commercial in the back of anyone's garage. The Production Company paid their costly location fee and we were very happy.

Lance Burton

Lance Burton is now one of the top names in magic. He stars in his own magic review at a gorgeous theatre that bears his name at the lavish Monte Carlo Hotel in Las Vegas. Lance tells the story of having driven from Tennessee to California in a beat-up, old car to appear on *It's Magic!* in 1981. At the time, he was an IBM Gold Medal Winner. I shared the stage with him at Tony Spina's Tannen's Jubilee in New York and offered him a spot on the show. Brother Bill had seen him at the IBM Convention and we both agreed he was a sensational new act. Lance says one afternoon he met me at the W.C. Fields Bar at the Variety Arts Theatre. (He was under twenty-one and I splurged and bought him a Coke.) According to Lance, I very casually told him we had booked him for a spot to plug *It's Magic!* show on the *Carson Show*. He said he'd be happy to do anything to help the show and then, after a long beat, said: "*The Carson Show*—you mean, the *Johnny Carson Show*!!!?"

The rest was history. Lance wowed 'em and Johnny had discovered another new talent. Lance appeared on the *Tonight Show* ten times over the Carson years. His magic star has been on a constant rise ever since. He's now up at the top with his new theatre and show in Las Vegas and his own TV specials, (thanks a great deal to his manager, Peter Reveen, who has proved he is *The Impossiblist* in more ways than one.) Lance closed his show in Las Vegas for a week in 1996 to perform in *It's Magic!* that year. It was Lance's way of saying "thank you" for our help in jump-starting his career.

Lights Out!

One April Fool's Day, about three in the afternoon, there was a huge clap of thunder and all the power went out. People don't realize it, but there are very few *real* windows in the Castle. This is because of security and air conditioning. Most of the windows you see are back-lit stained glass. Thus, dear friends, when the lights go out at the Castle, it gets real dark!

Our emergency lighting system is designed to light hallways, stairways and exits. If the place is filled with people the emergency system will allow our patrons to exit safely. When the power went off at 3 p.m. all those lights worked perfectly–but there were no people in the Castle except our hard working staff, who really didn't want to exit.

So, what do you do when the lights go out? You wait for them to come back on again! It was a great day for Tom Edison, Marconi and Ben Franklin. We live in a world dependent on electricity. When the power goes out there are no telephones, no lights, no computers, no blenders, no TV, no sound, no cash registers, AND Open Sesame doors won't work. Houdini can't return from the dead and even Invisible Irma can't play her piano.

But hey … it was only three o'clock. We've had power failures before. How long could they last? A few minutes–maybe an hour? Surely the power would be restored quickly.

Two hours later we were getting a little worried. That night we had 276 dinner reservations and two seances. If the power came back on at 5 p.m. it wouldn't be too much of a problem. Lots of people like their prime rib very rare! By 6 p.m. we knew we were in deep—trouble. Patrons were starting to arrive, the sun was setting and the emergency lighting system was starting to dim out. I went out into the world to buy anything that would make light. We were burning dozens of candles and using more batteries than a seven-year-old at Christmas.

It was very weird. The power was on at the Magic Hotel but it was off in my office in the apartment house next door. Don Damaskin's shop in the garage by the parking lot had power and the Yamashiro had power. The Roosevelt Hotel had lights but El Capitan and the Chinese Theatres were dark. Our little April Fool's Day prank was to send a couple of hundred unexpected dinner patrons up the hill to the Yamashiro.

It could have been a fun night if God hadn't invented slip-and-fall lawsuits and insurance companies. We finally decided to tell the kitchen and food service staff to go home if the power was still off at 8 p.m. It was and they went home. Our magicians came in ready to work and we had a nice visit at our candlelit bar.

Greg Wilson was ready with his high-tech sound and laser light show but it would have taken one helluva lot of "D" cells to get him going. At nine o'clock we decided to close and go home. I told Al Davis I'd make a classy sign on the computer but he reminded me that a felt pen might work better. It was the first time the Castle had been closed for a reason other than a holiday in over two decades! For the record, the power was restored at 2:30 a.m. April First was April Fool's Day. It was also Marvyn Roy's birthday. "Mr. Electric" where were you when we needed you?

President for Life

Unfortunately Bill's life was too short. He passed away February 1993, at the age of 64. Since this book is based on my columns in our Magic Castle® Friday lunch menus, and newsletters, these were my thoughts at the time of his passing:

"I somehow knew I would have to write this column someday. In recent months, my Brother Bill has been extremely ill, hospitalized and in and out of intensive care. But there was always hope for just one more miracle, just one greater bit of magic.

Yesterday morning at about 7 a.m., he shed his pain-wrecked body and took off on a journey to visit a number of dear, old friends. Dante, Virgil, Jay Ose, Blackstone, Sr., Dai Vernon and, especially the man he admired most in his lifetime, William W. Larsen, Sr. Bill thought he had a date to meet our father many years ago. Dad had died at a very early age, 48, and Bill really believed he wouldn't make fifty. He was amazed when he found himself in his fifties, much less his sixties. He said, in a recent *Genii* Speaks editorial: 'If I had known I was going to live this long, I would have taken better care of myself.' I think that was an old George Burns' line, but Bill always liked it.

My brother had no hobbies. He had two loves in his life, his family and magic. His love of his family always came first. (The family also includes the dogs, the cats, the squirrels, the blue jays, and the rest of the wildlife at the Larsen family home, Brookledge.)

The second love, magic, was his life. He had a wonderful obsession that the world would be a better place if it were populated with nothing but magicians. He would go to a convention and see every act, every show, every lecture and he knew every dealer. Bill was only 64 years old when he left us. He would have been 65, May 8th. I am three years younger. Bill liked to call himself, 'The grand old man of magic.' I preferred to call myself a 'kid that never grew up.' Since I was barely in my twenties when Dad left us, I thought of Bill as a combination brother and father.

In all those years that Bill and I worked together on many projects, including the Magic Castle® and *It's Magic!* we never once had an argument. We had 'discussions' ... Sometimes we didn't agree ... But we never had an argument. For two brothers in business together, that's something of a miracle in itself. We had a mutual love and respect for each other. We always kidded that he had no idea of what I did and I had no idea of what he did—we were a great team! Bill was an incredible human being. He had left this world having no enemies and thousands of friends. The Academy of Magical Arts, the Magic Castle® and *Genii* Magazine will all go on without Bill at the helm. The mark of a fine Captain is that he trained his crew well.

Bill and I were always proud of making Dad's dream for a social order for magicians come true. We often spoke of the idea that somehow Dad was enjoying his creation and that his presence could be felt every time a magician's act was applauded. Now Brother Bill will have a chance to ask him how he liked what his kids have done. He can also ask John Shrum how he likes what we've done to the new rooms. I'm in no hurry to join their meeting but to quote a line from one of Dad's obituaries in *Genii*: 'Someday we'll meet again, untrammeled by the physical. What a magical convention that will be.' So, aloha Bill, 'til we meet again."

Quoting again from a Friday lunch menu:
"On Sunday, May 2nd, 1993, Irene Larsen and the family and a few very close friends went for a short ocean voyage and Brother Bill, 'The Prez' became part of the most living thing on earth, the sea. Dr. John Booth said some beautiful words and Bill's ashes vanished among flower petals. It was a beautiful ceremony. Later that day, the Castle was jammed with members, relatives and friends, who stopped by to raise their glasses and to celebrate the life of Bill Larsen, Jr. It was a day of love, warmth and good cheer. It was exactly the way Bill wanted it."

I looked through some of the bound volumes of *Genii* Magazine to find some bits from Bill's editorials over the years to use in the short talk I delivered that day. There was too much to choose from so I simply ad-libbed my way through the speech, got a few pretty good chuckles, and asked Reverend Booth to repeat his earlier thoughts. Irene expressed a thousand thoughts with very few words and thanked those who had traveled great distances to be with us for Bill's 'wake.'

One of Bill's *Genii* editorials caught my eye. This goes back to the issue of November 1961. This is a quote: "Most exciting is the fact that the Magic Castle® Club is actually becoming a reality. Many of the more pessimistic, local magicians can't seem to believe that Brother Milt and his partners are willing to invest a small fortune in the belief that magicians and magical enthusiasts will support the art of magic. I predict it will be the biggest success ever associated with magic."

Bill should have been right up there with Nostradamus. There is no question that the Magic Castle brought a new life to the art of magic.

The entire history of the Magic Castle® and the Academy of Magical Arts is well recorded through a diary that has been kept for a generation. The diary is in the form of the newsletters, which go back to 1962, in which my late Brother Bill took pride in writing in the style of his personal letter to the membership of the Academy. He used the same style in writing his editorial, *Genii* Speaks, in *Genii* Magazine every month. Through the newsletter and *Genii*, the world of magic knew all about Bill, the Magic Castle®, Irene, their dogs and cats, his old station wagon and even his famous stuffed bear.

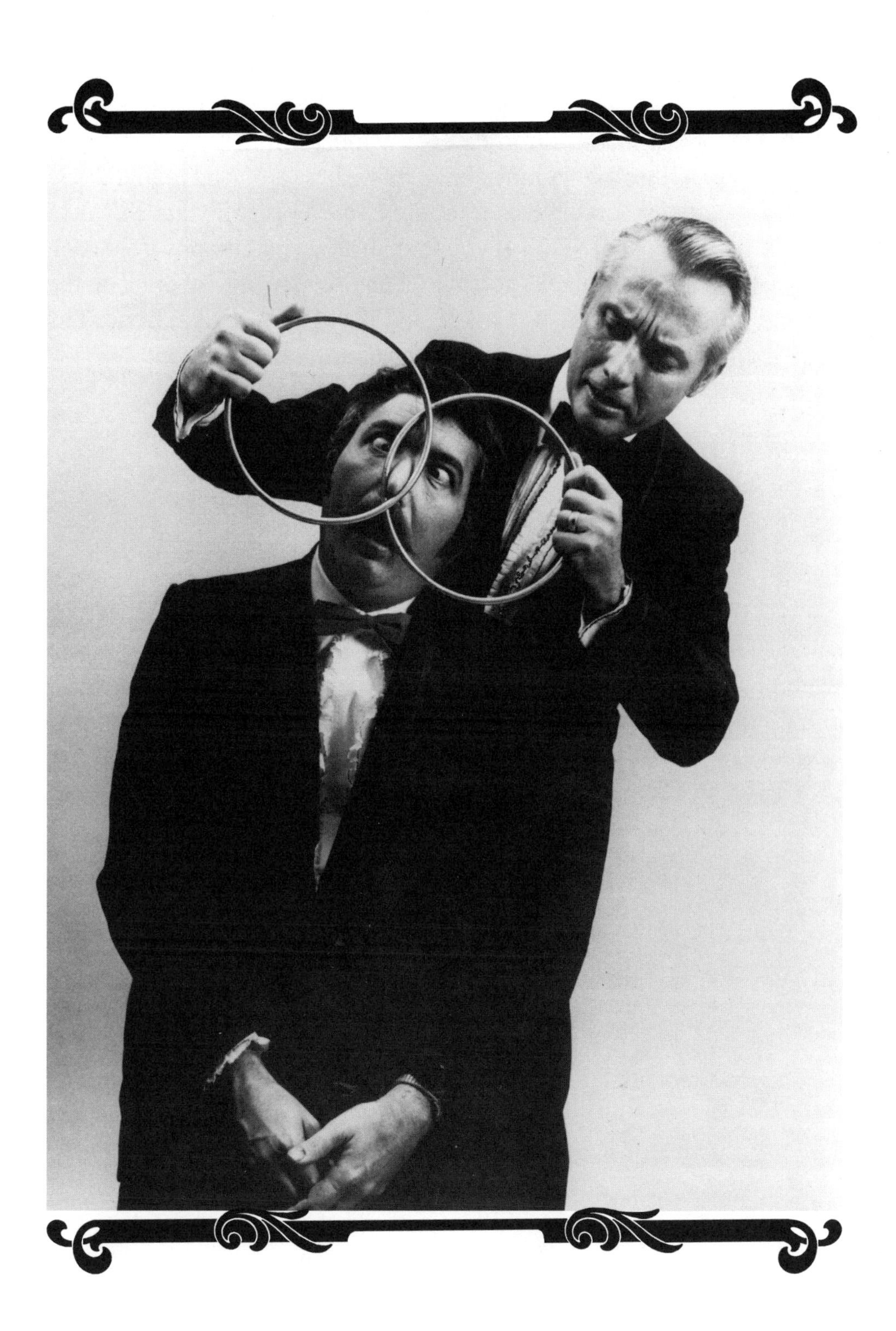

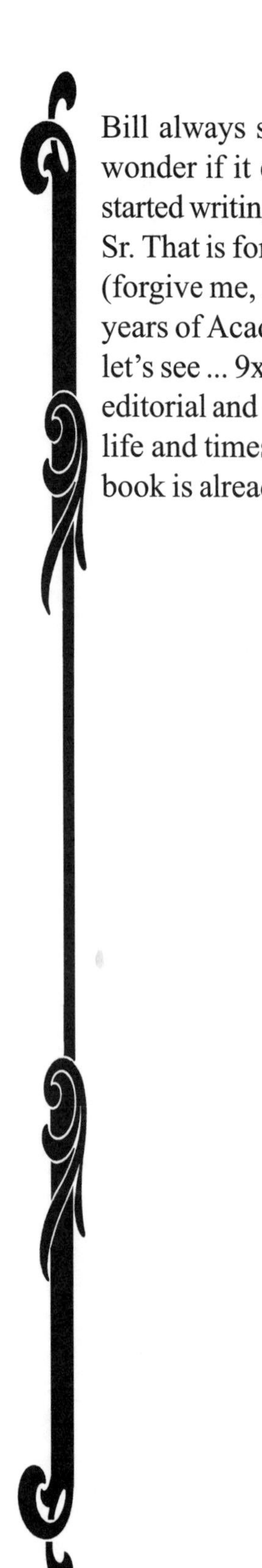

Bill always said he wanted to write a book about his life in magic. I wonder if it ever occurred to him that he has already written one. He started writing the *Genii* editorial in 1953 after the passing of Bill Larsen, Sr. That is forty years of editorials. By my most simplistic mathematics (forgive me, Arthur Benjamin), that's 624 editorials. Add to that thirty years of Academy Newsletters at roughly nine a year and that's ... uh ... let's see ... 9x30 ... that's 270. If you took just two paragraphs from each editorial and each newsletter you would have a nice big, fat book on the life and times of William W. Larsen, Jr. Okay Dante, Erika, Irene. The book is already written, all we need is an editor.

The Next Million Years

More Castles?

Armand Grant and I produced a number of magic specials for CBS and ABC-TV. One idea that got as far as a development deal (for un-initiated that means they pay you a bunch of money but the show never flies) we pitched a documentary on the history of magic. I always loved the title: "Magic, the First Million Years." I always said, "I wrote the Magic Castle®." I put together a scenario of adults going up to a magic owl and saying "Open Sesame" and then entering an *Alice in Wonder-land* place where magic was everywhere. Patrons became part of the act and even talked to an invisible piano player named Irma. The Magic Castle® was, and still is, the ultimate audience participation show. That's the secret of our little magical illusion.

Prior to the Magic Castle® magicians had no place to "magish."When the Magic Castle® opened in 1963 there was nothing like a venue devoted to magic. Going back to something that Ed Wynn might have said. He didn't... but he might have said: "A diamond is just a rock until it is cut and polished with glistening facets. Take that stone and encase it in a beautiful gold setting and then place it in a velvet box marked Tiffany. It's still the same rock, just a lot easier to sell. All we did was to take the great magic talent that was there and we gave the acts a beautiful setting. Of that we are very proud. No one really thought the Castle could become successful when we first started.

Even Bill and I figured the club would probably top out at about 500 members. If we had ever really done a feasibility study on the project it would simply not have been feasible.

We had faith in the idea and our good friends and members stood behind us at every turn. Over the years there have been a few imitators of the Castle concept. We have never considered other magic venues competition. For the most part we try to help and promote them. Even at seven magicians a week and fifty-two weeks a year we can't employ all of the world's magicians. In Southern California there are a number of excellent clubs and theaters offering magical entertainment. *WizardZ* at Universal City's "CityWalk," Mike Lacey's *Comedy and Magic Club* in Hermosa Beach, Steve Spill's *Magicopolis* and others.

Several years ago a club opened in Newport Beach about fifty miles south of Los Angeles. Instead of asking for our cooperation, the promoter was very vocal about the fact that the Magic Castle® was the Cadillac of magic but his club would be the Rolls Royce. He said the Castle had excellent amateurs but his new club would hire only the top professionals. In promoting the new club, which was patterned exactly like the Magic Castle®, he kept putting down the Castle. Bill and I resented this so Bill never mentioned the club in *Genii* Magazine. We encouraged our Castle magicians to perform there because they paid well. The general feeling was another comparison: The Newport Beach club was cold and elegant. The Magic Castle® was warm and friendly.

Even earlier, a group of magicians in Dallas, Texas asked if we would be interested in a Dallas Magic Castle®. We said we were not interested at the time but they had our blessing to do a club along the same lines as long as they didn't use our name. We gave them a great deal of help and let some of our people work with them on the project. For their opening night they invited a number of magicians as their guests including Bill and Irene Larsen, Milt Larsen and Dai Vernon. It was a fun party. On the way back we all agreed they blew it! Their close-up room had paper-thin walls and was next to the foot stomping western dance floor. Walk around magicians competed with loud music, beautiful ladies and pulsating lights. The club had a very short life.

Universal Studios decided they would like a Magic Castle® at their new CityWalk development. We talked to them about the idea of a Castle at the new park in Orlando, Florida. That would have been a perfect location for another Castle but Universal only wanted to pursue a Florida club if the Hollywood Castle was part of the deal. They argued that we could keep the existing Castle as a private club and open another Castle that would be for the public. We just couldn't see it and passed on the whole deal. The Universal CityWalk property is where *WizardZ* is now located and doing well enough that a new *WizardZ* has opened in Tokyo, Japan.

Caesar's Castle?

Over the years we had talked about the possibilities of other Magic Castles. We'd talked to people in New York, San Francisco and even Cleveland, Ohio. My good friend and TV producing associate Armand Grant and I talked to the folks at Caesar's Palace in Las Vegas and Atlantic City about thirty years ago with the idea of producing a Magic Castle-type experience in their showrooms. For whatever reasons all those plans didn't gel.

One sunny afternoon in 1992 I was crossing the street on Wilshire Boulevard and Rodeo Drive in Beverly Hills. We had just finished a rehearsal for our Academy of Magical Arts Awards Show at the Beverly Wilshire Hotel. I ran into Allen Bregman, an old friend who booked stars like Frank Sinatra and David Copperfield for Caesar's Palace (in fact, he was in charge of all entertainment for Caesar's World!) I mentioned that I'd like to set up a meeting to discuss a new idea that I thought would be great for Caesars. I didn't really get into the idea, but it involved a new concept I had for a slot machine oriented audience participation game and show. Allen said he'd set up a meeting.

The next thing I knew I was having lunch in a posh Century City restaurant with Allen Bregman, a couple other key Caesar's executives and Henry Gluck, the Chairman of the Board of Caesar's World. (Henry, incidentally, is the brother of Richard M. Sherman's wife, Ursula. Academy Award-winning songwriter, Richard, is one of my dearest friends and collaborators. Hollywood is a small world, after all.) After the usual pleasantries, Henry asked why we were all having lunch? I hauled out my presentation boards for my new game idea and started my pitch.

Henry Gluck didn't become one of the nation's top business executives for nothing. He very nicely, but very abruptly, ended my presentation by explaining that new games were difficult if not impossible to create in Las Vegas. Then he explained they all thought I wanted to talk about magic. I quickly put my game idea aside and we started talking about the idea of a Magic Castle-type venue in Las Vegas. We all agreed that intimate magic was lacking in Las Vegas. The greatest magicians in the world play there. Siegfried and Roy, David Copperfield, Lance Burton—all dazzling with big stage magic but there is really no place for the close-up and other intimate styles of magic associated with the Magic Castle®.

Henry Gluck cut to the quick: "Show we can create an attraction with intimate magic, give people fabulous intimate magicians, and entertain guests for intimate dinner and shows … and put 2,500 people through the place every day of the week … and we'll build it!"

I didn't have the immediate answer. Obviously the Magic Castle® as a private club with Victorian atmosphere wouldn't work. Nor would just shows and smaller show rooms as we had once discussed. We needed a gimmick and Henry and Allen agreed they'd buy me another lunch if I could come up with an answer. What a wonderful challenge.

I actually came up with the idea driving back to the Magic Castle® from the Caesar's World offices in Century City. Anyone who has ever written for network TV knows you can't make creativity appear to be that easy. I mentioned my friend Richard M. Sherman earlier in this story. Dick and his brother Robert wrote many of this country's biggest hits including the Oscar winning score for Walt Disney's *Mary Poppins, Chitty Chitty Bang Bang,* and one of the most played songs of all time, Disney's *It's a Small World After All*. Someone asked Dick how long it took to write one of their famous songs. His answer was "all my life." He explained, "It may only take a few moments to write down a tune or a lyric or an idea, but it takes the experiences and the knowledge of a lifetime to create magic combinations.

I had the answer to Henry's challenge by the time I got back to my office. It was an idea so pure and simple that it had to work. I waited a few discrete days and then called Henry. "I think I've found the answer to your challenge ... Is it worth another lunch?"

I met with the same group at the same restaurant and, after the same pleasantries, I told them: "After our meeting I went back to the Magic Castle® library and spent the next few days pouring over magical history, especially from the days of the Roman Empire. I came up with something so exciting that I almost called everybody at midnight to yell it to the housetops. Did you know Julius Caesar was so impressed with the abilities of the magicians of his empire that he built a hidden city beneath Rome where the magicians could live and enjoy the finest fruits of life. He entertained his most precious guests in his hidden city and, by so doing, controlled the magicians, who might have been a danger to him politically. There is a rumor that this city still exists in the buried ruins. What if we could find it and rebuilt it in Las Vegas?"

Henry Gluck's eyes lit up. He asked me if that was true. I said if he believed it for just a moment, it must be true. Besides, there are very few people living now who are two thousand years old. He loved it.

Henry gave the green light to the project and I was hired as Magical Consultant. I wrote an outline of the hidden city experience as I saw it. Then the incredible team from Landmark Entertainment took over to make it all happen in a way I could never have imagined. They gave a new meaning to the phrase *first class*. Throughout the Empire you see gimmicks that remind you of the Magic Castle®. A barstool sinks, a table revolves and an invisible pianist plays. There's an intimate dining experience in fabulous dining chambers deep in the catacombs and two beautiful showrooms modeled after the ones at the Magic Castle®. Las Vegas being Las Vegas it's a little more *theme park* than our warm cozy Castle, but it's really something to see. At this writing the Caesar's is once again under new ownership and the executives at Park Place Entertainment seem to be very happy with the Empire.

Shortly after work was started on the forty million dollar project, Caesar's World was sold to the Sheraton Hotel chain. Henry Gluck went on to other projects and Allen Bregman suffered a stroke. I remained as consultant for the four years of construction and the opening. I am very proud to have been associated with Caesar's Magic Empire.

A final word as we go to press with this book I wrote another Friday lunch menu story August 25, 2000 that really should be included with respect to the above: The Rise and Fall of Caesar's Magical Empire. I just got a call from Tom Pinkerton from Park Place Entertainment. He was responding to a call I had made to Mike Leonard, the marketing VP of Park Place. I had a meeting with Mike a few months ago about a plan that I thought might solve a few of their concerns about Caesar's Magical Empire.

When I was at the FISM Congress of Magic in Lisbon last month, one of the most frequently asked questions was about the status of the Magic Empire. Since I was the guy that created the Empire, magicians assumed I knew all the answers. Sadly, Tom Pinkerton confirmed the fact that Caesar's will close in two or three months to make way for a new huge nightclub. That seems to be the latest trend in Las Vegas where multi-million dollar projects come and go as fast as fry cooks at McDonalds. Caesar's used to be the classiest hotel/casino in Las Vegas where shirts and tank tops were a rarity. Apparently, the high rollers of today are the club scene crowd, giving a new meaning to the word *high*.

The closing of the Empire is tragic because I firmly believe it could have been a major attraction in Las Vegas with proper marketing and a few simple changes. I asked Tom if he had seen the letter I sent Mike Leonard outlining those changes and he said he had not. I assume the idea was killed in an earlier meeting of Park Place's lower brass. I can't believe Park Place Entertainments CEO, Arthur Goldberg, wouldn't have wanted to spend a half-hour with a guy with a plan to save the company forty million bucks. (A guy with a fabulous private theater in his home can't be all bad.)

In the meantime, Caesar's Magical Empire is still there for another couple of months. My wife, Arlene, and her relatives practically filled one of the dining chambers a couple of weeks ago and had a great time. Her gang all said the experience was well worth the money. (Yes, they paid to get in!)

In the words of John Greenleaf Whittier: "For of all sad words of tongue and pen, the saddest are these: *It might have been*." Hail Caesar! Et tu, Brute!

Franchising the Magic Castle

Readers of *Genii* Magazine and the Castle Newsletter will remember that the rumor of a second Magic Castle® would come up once in a while. A number of our New York members encouraged us to look into the possibility of a venue in the Big Apple and we got very serious about the idea in the late sixties.

I found a few available sites but deals didn't gel. At one point, I thought I had found the perfect location. It was a four-story early President's townhouse in the heart of Manhattan. In later years, it had been a restaurant. We opened some preliminary lease negotiations. Then I got a call from a very good friend who was a magician and very high up in the New York banking circles. He asked if I really knew with whom I was dealing? He expounded that the lease would bind us for whatever the length of that lease might be. But, if the owners wanted to break the lease, they would be able to do it with a telephone call. He said something about cement overshoes and the East River. We decided to pass on the location.

We also announced plans to open a Magic Castle® in San Francisco and even went so far as to publish photos of a couple of locations. Again we dropped the plans for one reason or another. One thing that always entered into our final thinking was that the Magic Castle® was a very personal family project. It was our child. We never wanted to franchise and have little imitation Castles stamped out with cookie cutters. If there were ever to be another Castle, it would have to be based on the same integrity and love of magic that has been the key to the success of the Hollywood Castle. Yes, there could be, and possibly will be, a second Magic Castle®, but it would have to have its own personality. That was, and is, always the goal if there should ever be another Magic Castle®.

Imitators have come and gone and the reason for their failure has always been the same. The investors always put the love of the dollar above the love of the art of magic and magicians.

How could we possibly put together the events, people and places to recreate the Magic Castle®? There can only be one Hollywood Illusion, a unique place where the guests are encouraged to join in the love of magic.

Backward

If there is such thing as a forward to a book, it seems to me there should also be a "backward." I mentioned at the outset that my editor would create deadlines and make life unbearable for a writer who really can't stop writing. As we go to press there are so many stories that still need to be told. There are people who have done major things to make the Magic Castle a success. A good example is the fact that the back cover of this book shows a great photo of the new Fountania fountain in front of the Castle. The people that made that all happen are a story that should be in this book but aren't. It's a great story about the front of the Castle by Joe Hoffman and Clark James. It will be in the next book!

There are great stories about one of our members Earl Witscher, and his son Don, who have contributed so much to the success of the Magic Castle. There is Bill Chaudet, K. C. Growe and Dr. Harry Seagal who were members before we numbered twenty and they still come in almost every Friday for lunch. There should be more about our landlords Tom and Jane Glover and Tom's mother Lucy. How about my old buddy George Falcon, new It's Magic! partner, Terry Hill, Arlene's family and friends? It will all have to wait. The Barracuda is going to get this book off to the printer.

There are hundreds of people I should thank for being with us all these years. If I missed a favorite story here and there I am very sorry. In almost forty years of hanging out at the Magic Castle I have made thousands of new friends and watched new talents develop through the opportunities provided through this very unique club.

Thank you for making this Hollywood Illusion into a major magical reality.

To paraphrase the legendary George M. Cohan who always said in his curtain speech: "My Father thanks you. My mother thanks you. My brother thanks you. And I thank you." — I simply thank you for making our Larsen family's impossible dream come true.